Robert Cazimero and Hālau Nā Kamalei

Men of Hula

Published and distributed by

ISLAND HERITAGE™
PUBLISHING

94-411 Kō'aki Street, Honolulu, Hawai'i 96797-2806
Orders: (800) 468-2800 • Information: (808) 564-8800
Fax: (808) 564-8877

islandheritage.com

ISBN: 1-59700-623-8
2nd Edition, First Printing—2011

©2010 Island Heritage Publishing. All rights reserved.
No portion of this book may be reproduced in whole or in part
in any form or by any means without prior written permission
from Island Heritage Publishing. Printed in Hong Kong.

Robert Cazimero and Hālau Nā Kamalei

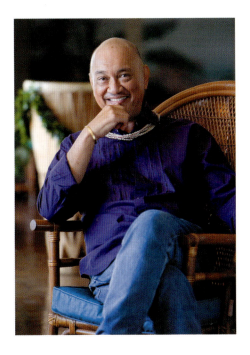

Written by **Benton Sen**

CONTENTS

	STATEMENT	7
	ACKNOWLEDGMENTS	8
	INTRODUCTION	11
CHAPTER 1	KŪ I KA MANA	12
CHAPTER 2	IN THE BEGINNING, THERE WAS HULA	15
CHAPTER 3	ONE LEGEND INSPIRES ANOTHER	22
CHAPTER 4	MEN WHO DANCE	30
CHAPTER 5	RENAISSANCE MEN	36
	The Brothers Cazimero	39
	Starting Out	39
	The Sweet Scent of Lei Day	41
	The Gift That Continues Giving	43
	The Renaissance of Hawaiian Pride	44
CHAPTER 6	KAHIKO, THE OLD SCHOOL	52
	Mary Kawena Pukuʻi	52
	Kauʻi Zuttermeister	54
	George Lanakilakekiahialiʻi Naʻope	57
CHAPTER 7	ʻAUANA, THE NEW SCHOOL	60
	Maiki Aiu Lake	60
	Wayne Wai Keahi Chang	63
	Leinaʻala Kalama Heine	65

CHAPTER 8	ROBERT CAZIMERO THEN	70
CHAPTER 9	ROBERT CAZIMERO NOW	74
CHAPTER 10	THE MERRIE MONARCH FESTIVAL SWAYS THE HEART OF HULA	80
CHAPTER 11	THE GENTLEMEN OF HĀLAU NĀ KAMALEI	86
	'Ohana	86
	Brad Cooper	87
	Kaipo Hale	89
	Manu Boyd	91
	Kyle Atabay	93
	Stanley Cadinha, Jr.	95
	Keola Makaiau	97
	Frank Among	99
	Alexander Parker	101
	Keala Chock	103
	Keo Woolford	104
	Kaulana Vares	107
CHAPTER 12	THE WORLD COMES TO HULA	110
CHAPTER 13	HULA IS LIFE	115
	BIBLIOGRAPHY	122
	ABOUT THE AUTHOR	124

Hula expresses everything we see, feel, hear, smell, taste, and touch. *Hula* is life.
—Robert Cazimero

ACKNOWLEDGMENTS

This book would not have been possible without the help of many. For their knowledge and inspiration, I would like to thank Lisette Marie Flanary whose film documentary about Robert Cazimero and Hālau Nā Kamalei provided insight for this book; Waimea Williams, for her editorial magic; and Tom Chapman and Brett Uprichard, for allowing me to write an article for *Spirit of Aloha* magazine on which this book is based.

I would also like to thank the many writers whose work appear in *Men of Hula*: Wanda Adams, Rita Ariyoshi, Shari Berinobis, Jess Blumberg, Catherine Enomoto, Lisette Marie Flanary, Constance Hale, Wayne Harada, Jerry Hopkins, George Kanahele, Mary Klarr, Aukai Reynolds, Ronn Ronck, Allan Seiden, Kalena Silva, Amy Kuʻuleialoha Stillman, Jon Woodhouse, and Keo Woolford.

A special mahalo to the Kalihi-Palama Culture and Arts Society for their books, *Nānā I Nā Loea Hula: Look to the Hula Resources*, Vol. 1 and Vol. 2, from which several interviews were taken.

Photographers contributing to *Men of Hula* include Romeo Collado, Wayne Iha, Hawaiʻi State Archives. Special thanks also go to Jon de Mello and Leah Bernstein of The Mountain Apple Company, Roland Cazimero, and The Brothers Cazimero who provided the personal family albums for selections of images included in this book.

I am indebted to the following for sharing their kindness, friendship, and food: Mark Ono, Andrew Brennan, John Lin, Willice Kealoha, Marie Smith, Connie Florez, Susan Kam Yokoyama, Edward Moore, Daniel Kleinknecht, Phil Willet, Michael Hoffman, and Richard Potter.

For their love and belief in me, I wish to thank my parents, Ben and Amy Sen, my sisters, Vena and Rhona, my nephews, Mat, Taylor, Justin, Brendon, and the source of all things good—H.P.

The final names on this list belong to Dale Madden and Island Heritage Publishing, and especially, the men of *hula* whose wisdom, generosity, and *aloha* inspire us all—Robert Cazimero and Hālau Nā Kamalei.

INTRODUCTION

In 1966 a major shift occurred in the practice of *hula*. The beginnings were modest but over time they created a revolution. The vision of one young man eventually brought about a permanent change in how Hawai'i's famous dances were practiced both at home and abroad. Robert Cazimero, at the time a recent Kamehameha Schools graduate, said that he felt led to a master teacher. She showed him a world that had been closed off to anyone then living: the world that belonged to the men of *hula*. This is the story of how ancient traditions were restored after being driven underground for nearly two hundred years. Hālau Nā Kamalei, the school founded and still guided by Robert Cazimero, is the only male *hālau hula* in the Hawaiian Islands.

Join us on this exciting and reverent journey into a realm that was almost lost forever.

CHAPTER 1

KŪ I KA MANA

▸▸

*H*ula is grounded in the cultural practices of our *kūpuna*, the elders of Hawaiian society. One statement that sums up this view is, *Kū i ka mana*. Translations vary but the basic meaning is, Be upright in spirit.

Like the master from whom Robert Cazimero received his instructions as *haumana*, student, he learned the traditions of his ancestors. Yet studying was, and still is, not just confined to one area like *hula*. True learning implies that through practice, discipline, and respect, a student can reflect the reverence that Hawaiians have for their people, their land, and their heritage. Among many things, *hula* gives its interpreters a sense of place and a sense of belonging. For all of us, the greatest sense of place is located deep within ourselves.

Kūpuna often quote *ʻolelo noʻeau*, ancient sayings. These are meant as guides to life and have been handed down for generations. Every beginning dancer will probably hear this saying at the first lesson:

ʻAʻa i ka hula, waiho ka hilahila i ka hale. Dare to *hula*, and leave shyness at home. This is a reminder that dancing requires a combination of nerve, skill, training, and patience. These words became the motto of Hālau Nā Kamalei.

Robert Cazimero began his career with six high school students. More than thirty years later the men of Hālau Nā Kamalei continue the tradition of male *hula*, which they revived. "There are times when I don't want to get up and dance," Robert says, "but sometimes, you have to leave the shame behind and forget what the guy over there is thinking." By blazing their journey with Hawaiian pride and dispelling deep-rooted stereotypes of grass-skirted girls with coconut bras, Hālau Nā Kamalei reclaimed the masculine side of ancient dance. "Above all, I know this to be truer than true," Robert believes. "We can all be made better for daring to dance."

The tie of ancient Hawaiian *hula* to martial art practice is reflected below in an early Hālau Nā Kamalei dance.

CHAPTER 2

IN THE BEGINNING, THERE WAS HULA

The source of *hula* is linked to a *pahu*, a drum named Hāwea. It was the original ancient accompaniment for dance, along with chanting, and it came to Hawai'i from a great distance. The drum was probably similar to those still made from the trunk of a coconut tree covered with stretched shark skin. This strong instrument produces powerful sounds. Under ideal conditions the tones of a large *pahu* can carry from one valley to the next. Little is now known about the details of Hāwea's arrival in the islands, but the drum is part of a famous chant that records the deeds of early settlers.

This chant was composed by the navigator Kamahualele. Most likely more than a thousand years ago he sailed by canoe with High Chief Mo'ikeha from Tahiti to Hawai'i and back. Eventually Mo'ikeha returned to Hawai'i but he left behind his infant son La'amaikahiki, and the drum Hāwea. On the next journey across 2,800 miles of open ocean, the navigator sighted Mauna Kea and Mauna Loa, and traveled on to Kaua'i. There he recited the chant that begins,

> *Eia Hawai'i, he moku he kanaka!*
>
> Behold Hawai'i, an island, a people!
>
> *He kanaka e!*
>
> A people indeed!

Herb Kāne's painting depicts the ancient Polynesian voyagers first discovery of the Hawaiian Islands.

He kanaka Hawaiʻi, He kama na Kahiki…

The nation of Hawaiʻi is a child of Tahiti…

When Moʻikeha reached Wailua Nui Hōʻano, Kauaʻi's great sacred river, he saw two daughters of the island's ruling chief. They became his wives and after their father died, Moʻikeha succeeded him as ruling chief. However, decades and thousands of miles could not break family ties. In his later years Moʻikeha sent his Hawaiian-born son, Kila, to Tahiti to find Laʻamaikahiki, the son he had left behind. To locate him, Kila was told to follow the powerful sound of a drum. Kila found both the son and the drum, and returned to Hawaiʻi with both of them.

Laʻamaikahiki beat his *pahu* as their canoe sailed along the coasts of the islands. As if hearing the beating of their own hearts, people ran to the shores and showered the travelers with gifts. At Hanauma Bay on Oʻahu, a man named Haikamalama followed the canoe and mimicked the drum's rhythm by slapping his chest, and repeated the chant until he had learned it. As the canoe approached Kauaʻi, Moʻikeha recognized Laʻamaikahiki from the sound of his *pahu*. After they were reunited, Laʻamaikahiki became famous. The long-absent son traveled from island to island, teaching *hula* and chants, accompanied by his legendary drum.

"The Hawaiians were great poets," says Maiki Aiu Lake, revered *kupuna* and Robert Cazimero's *kumu hula*, his master teacher. "Nature provided them with sounds of the wind, rain, surf, bubbling streams, waterfalls, birdcalls, rustling leaves—all of these sounds and more. They chanted of their thoughts as they experienced life itself, of their feelings of ambition, jealousy, sexual behavior, romantic love, parental love, these and more. Also recorded was their attitude toward their superiors, *aliʻi*, their great deeds, their battles, the mysteries of their *ʻaumakua*. All of these may be found in the endless *oli* (chants), *mele* (songs), *pule* (prayers)."

According to other sources, there were originally two gods of *hula*, one male and one female. Unbounded and ethereal, they communed with deities and the spirits of nature, and were able to travel in time. After arriving from Kahiki, also called Tahiti, these two gods danced for the Hawaiian people. Their chants and movements were called *hula*. However, both deities claimed to have created it. To solve the dispute they challenged each other to dance from day into night, as the sun rose and evening fell. They danced while chanting above the sounds of the surf, and among the winds in the forest. Without rest they leaned, swayed, and turned, and because of their unceasing momentum the two gods merged into one body, one breath. When at last there was stillness, only the female form remained: Laka, goddess of *hula*.

Still another tradition records *hula* as originally reserved for men, and ruled over by a male god named Laka. The rigorous training and athletic components of dance made it an ideal training ground for young warriors. Today *hula* is divided into *kahiko,* ancient style, and *'auana,* a post-contact or modern style that continues to develop in present time. The roots of *hula* in the distant past are reflected in chants passed down over generations. Many of these describe battles, triumphant warrior chiefs, and warfare in which gods and powerful animals play a significant role. Such *hula* have specific moves and gestures that demonstrate fighting stances.

Despite this male exclusivity, in one legend Hi'iaka, the youngest sister of the fire goddess Pele, learned to dance from Laka. Hi'iaka taught her new skill to her best friend Hopoe, a poet, on the beach at Nanahuki. Pele heard Hi'iaka chanting and was pleased because of her own memories of dancing on the beach with Hopoe. After that, it was said to be common for women as well as men to learn and perform *hula.* This first known *hula* chant is rich with place names and nature references.

> *Ke ha'a la Puna i ka makani*
> Puna dances in the breeze
> *Ha'a ka ulu hala i Kea'au*

While pandanus trees shake in Kea'au

Ha'a Ha'ena me Hopoe.

Ha'ena and Hopoe dance.

Ha'a ka wahine

The woman dances

'Ami i kai o Nanahuki la.

Swaying close by the sea at Nanahuki.

Hula lea wale

The dance is most pleasing

I kai o Nanahuki, e'e!

Close by the sea at Nanahuki!

'O Puna kai kowa i ka hala

Puna's voice echoes in the pandanus trees

Pa'e ka leo o ke kai

Sounding like the distant sea.

Ke lu la i na pua lehua

The lehua blooms are blown away

Nana i kai o Hopoe

Hopoe is dancing near the sea

Ka wahine 'ami i kai

The woman is swaying

'O Nanahuki la,

By the sea at Nanahuki,

Hula le'a wale

The dance is most pleasing

I kai o Nanahuki e'e!

Close by the sea at Nanahuki!

One of the most revered Hawaiian love stories is also the most famous *hula* myth. In this long epic, dance has a prominent part in the love triangle of Pele, Hiʻiaka, and Lohiʻau, a handsome chief from Kauaʻi. It begins happily. After Hiʻiaka's dear friend Hopoe, her *hoaloha*, danced the first known *hula* on the shores of Nanahuki, Pele planted an *ʻōhiʻa* forest in Hiʻiaka's honor. One day some time later Pele's spirit left her body and floated to Kauaʻi. At the *hula heiau*, temple, in Haʻena, Pele fell in love with Chief Lohiʻau. She transformed herself into a beautiful woman and remained with him for several days of dancing and feasting. When Pele returned to her body in Kīlauea crater, she asked her sisters to bring Lohiʻau from Kauaʻi to live with her in the volcano. Only Hiʻiaka agreed to undertake the dangerous journey. For her efforts, Pele promised to protect Hopoe and to guard Hiʻiaka's *ʻōhiʻa* forest.

When Hiʻiaka finally reached Kauaʻi she discovered that Lohiʻau had died of grief over Pele's departure. Using many prayers, Hiʻiaka returned him to life. Pele suspected her youngest sister of seducing Lohiʻau, and blazed with revenge. At Kīlauea, the fire goddess faced Puna and raised her arms. The ground shook and Pele's anger flowed in lava streams through Hiʻiaka's *ʻōhiʻa* forest. Pele then cast her gaze on Hopoe's house on the beach at Nanahuki. As the lava approached it, Hopoe danced in defiance at the edge of the ocean. She continued to dance beyond hope of escape, swaying until Pele turned her into stone. The fate of Hiʻiaka and Lohiʻau was equally dramatic. When they returned to the Big Island of Hawaiʻi and the scene of Pele's devastation, they declared their love for each other and met with a fiery death.

Roland Cazimero's song, "Hiʻiaka's Pledge," is her promise to Pele that she will not betray her sacred mission. Hiʻiaka will find Lohiʻau and return him safely to Kīlauea. This pledge is the embodiment of tradition, love, and the spirit of *hula*.

> Not caring what befalls me, for I love you,
> Pain and sorrow
> Will not hinder my way.
> I'm to bring back the lover of Pele
> Lohiʻau is his name.
>
> She will see me through
> Make my path so clear.
>
> From Hawaiʻi I come to fetch him
> To sit at my sister's side once more.
> Obstacles and trials may befall me
> But I will endure.
>
> She chose me, for there was no other,
> No other that could stand the strain
> I am Hiʻiaka, I am Pele, Pele's flame
> I am Hiʻiakaikapoliopele.

CHAPTER 3

ONE LEGEND INSPIRES ANOTHER

▰▰▰▰▰▰▰▰▰▰▰▰▰▰▰▰▰▰▰▰▰▰▰▰▰▰

For many, there is a defining moment when the search for discovery leads you back to yourself. For Robert Cazimero this occurred in 1966. In that year he was introduced to a teacher who would instruct him in the ways of *hula*. He believes that nothing happens by accident. Quite simply, he was meant to be the student of this particular master.

"In high school, I met my *kumu hula*, Maiki Aiu Lake," Robert says.

"As she left the class that she had come to speak with, which was the class we were in, she told me: 'You know, someday you will want to teach *hula*, and you'll want to take *hula*, and I'm going to be that teacher.' Then years later, I found myself at her door of her school. I went to her '*hula* university.'"

Robert started his *hālau* with six students from the Kamehameha Schools.

A decade later in 1975, Maiki Aiu Lake had a very unusual request for her *haumana*, Robert Cazimero. He should become a teacher himself, for male dancers. This was highly significant and a landmark change for the *hula* community. Robert started his group with six students from the Kamehemeha Schools. Later he was joined by Wayne Chang, a graduate of Maiki's second class, and they founded the first male *hālau* of the modern era. They asked their respected and beloved teacher for a name. She chose

Nā Kamalei o Lililehua, which they eventually shortened to Nā Kamalei, the *lei* of children.

The two men soon made another name for themselves. Just one year later in 1976, they brought Nā Kamalei to the prestigious Merrie Monarch *Hula* Festival, the world-renowned competition on the Big Island. It was the first time that the *kāne* (men's) division was introduced to the festival. Nā Kamalei walked away with the overall *kāne 'auana* (men's contemporary) award.

The arrival of Hālau Nā Kamalei signaled the departure from *hula* as it was usually performed. Some critics argued that the new *hālau* showed no reverence for the past. They called Robert and his dancers too modern, and said that they had strayed too far from traditional styles. Robert's position was that the evolution of Hawaiian dance did not stop with the death of Kalākaua in 1891. "Today," he says, "the *hula* is not frozen in time but very much alive."

Nevertheless, this reasonable approach created turmoil. Robert says he loved incorporating elements of ballet and modern dance, and merging them into his *hula* choreography. "I would get a lot of static for being too avant-garde and became one of the 'rebels' of the time," he recalls. "When I think of what people were doing then, compared to what people are doing now, it was a breakthrough time. It has validated who I am today."

In the mid- to late-70s when Robert first blended classic with contemporary *hula*, and began mixing in elements of Western dance, "purists" were not happy. Several times his group was disqualified in competitions because of its controversial style. When asked to describe his approach to choreography, Robert backs away from the word sexy and prefers to call it manly grace. In fact, *hālau* members are known as The Gentlemen of Nā

Robert on the left, *kumu hula* Maiki Aiu Lake, and Wayne Chang.

Kamalei. Today Robert says, "Since 1975, many changes have taken place. "Wayne is no longer with me, talented dancers have come and gone, a few original members remain, and the dance continues." He considers talent to be a God-given gift, and that it is also what Auntie Maiki Aiu Lake gave him. Years later she is never far from his mind. A mention of her name brought this recent reply:

"I always used to say to her that I would never be here if it weren't for you, and she said, 'No, that's not true. You have the talent, it's a God-given talent, and what I've been able to do is bring out the talent that is in you and make it flourish. It doesn't always work. If you can find one or two in your lifetime, then you are a lucky person.' I told her, 'You are a very lucky person, because there are quite a few of us,' and she said, 'You will find that, too,' and I have. The male *hālau* was her dream. I loved her so much, I would have done anything she asked of me."

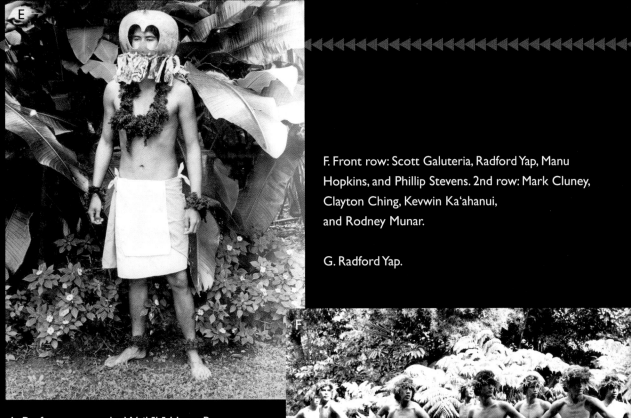

F. Front row: Scott Galuteria, Radford Yap, Manu Hopkins, and Phillip Stevens. 2nd row: Mark Cluney, Clayton Ching, Kevwin Kaʻahanui, and Rodney Munar.

G. Radford Yap.

A. Performance at the Waikīkī Hyatt Regency.

B. Home at Pumehana in Pūpūkea, early 70s. Robert Cazimero and Wayne Wai Chang.

C. *Hālau* rehearsal at Pumehana.

D. Reginald Keaunui III, Paul Luckey in back.

E. Rodney Munar.

CHAPTER 4

MEN WHO DANCE

>For many of us, hula conjures up visions of slender Hawaiian women in leafy skirts, coconut bras, and plastic leis. Think Blue Hawai'i, a 1961 Elvis movie, or the Brady Bunch's ill-fated trip to the islands, complete with a tiki curse and Alice in a grass skirt.
>
>—Jess Blumberg, Smithsonian Magazine

In ancient Hawai'i, reverence for *hula* was a sacred practice in which music, dance, and poetry described the genealogy and legends of the Hawaiian people. Through oral tradition, regarded as the highest form of spiritual and artistic expression, stories about the gods were passed on. In the 1800s, sentiment gave way to resentment. When the missionaries arrived in Hawai'i, they brought puritanical Calvinist values that drastically countered traditional island society. *Hula* was banned as too erotic. Worshipping Hawaiian gods was condemned.

According to Robert Cazimero, *hula* was an important part of religion, another reason why it was abolished. "Many of the teachers went into hiding," he says. The ban lasted for fifty years until the laws were lifted in the early 1870s. When David Kalākaua was elected king in 1874, a revival redefined the dance and returned it to its rightful place in the past. For the next seventeen years, Kalākaua, known as the Merrie Monarch, brought elegance and tradition back to the Hawaiian people.

During his reign, Kalākaua became the first Hawaiian king to visit the United States. He built 'Iolani Palace, the only royal residence on American soil, and he planned for Hawai'i to become an independent nation. However, Kalākaua will forever be remembered as the Merrie Monarch, the king who brought back the *hula*, and a true Hawaiian renaissance man. Samuel Crowningburg-Amalu, a

>Hula is the language of the heart, therefore the heartbeat of the Hawaiian people.
>—King David Kalākaua

Kalākaua will forever be remembered as the Merrie Monarch, the king who brought back the *hula*.

Nā Kamalei performing in traditional costume.

Native Hawaiian writer, described him in the *Honolulu Advertiser*: "Kalākaua dreamed of elegance in his little court at 'Iolani and to house that court, he erected a new palace, bought crowns to grace his head, created new medallions to begem his breast, and a new protocol to enhance his throne. King Kalākaua turned the eyes of his people away from their own provincial and insular past. He gave them the world. He brought the Hawaiian people out of a simple yesterday and promised them a bright and sophisticated tomorrow. Almost single-handedly he created the romance that somehow to this very day has never quite departed from the Hawaiian Islands. At exactly the right time that he was most needed, this prince of dreams was there."

The peak of Kalākaua's reign occurred in 1883 when he held coronation celebrations for himself and Queen Kapi'olani. He invited seven of Hawai'i's foremost *kumu hula* and their *hālau* to perform. The repertoire featured the contemporary style of *hula 'auana* along with *hula kahiko* (ancient style), combining the best of both worlds. Over several days more than two hundred sixty chants and dances were presented for the royal couple and their many guests.

Queen Kapi'olani.

The great success of these festivities was echoed three years later. In 1886, for the King's Jubilee on his fiftieth birthday, *hula* events seen by thousands lasted for two weeks. The following year in 1887, another *hula* celebration commemorated Kalākaua's return to the islands after a two-week trip. His support of music and dance rescued many ancient compositions by recording them for posterity, and it also opened *hula* to new styles and foreign influences that appealed to the king. At court, ladies and gentlemen performed the latest *hula* in the elabo-

A two-week *hula* celebration was held for King Kalākaua's fiftieth birthday.

rate fashions of the time. New steps were developed. New songs were welcomed. Today, Kalākaua's contributions to preserving Hawaiian culture and *hula* are memorialized in the world-class Merrie Monarch Festival held annually in Hilo. He is considered a renaissance man, one equally gifted in the fields of  politics, diplomacy, languages, and the arts and sciences. However, after the king's death in 1891, and the overthrow of the monarchy in 1893, *hula* performed for and by the royal court came to an end. Hawaiian culture nearly came to an end as well. For both male and female teachers and dancers, *hula* entered a period of repression and artificiality. This lasted for the next seven decades.

CHAPTER 5

RENAISSANCE MEN

From Shirley Temple strumming an ʻukulele to Hilo Hattie doing the Hilo Hop, stereotypes threatened to become the cultural norm for hula.

After the Hawaiian Kingdom crumbled, after the Territorial period, World War II, after Elvis, statehood, the Beatles, and Vietnam, the late 1960s sent the nation into the throes of the Civil Rights movement. The demand for self-determination stirred other minorities to join in. In Hawaiʻi the face of society changed to challenge the "melting pot" notion that everyone should be like everyone else. "Blacks were fighting for the right to equality on the mainland," Robert Cazimero says. "In Hawaiʻi, we were inspired by other people of color to seek that same kind of recognition and sense of equality for ourselves."

The winds of change blew through the islands in the 1970s with a cultural resurgence that came to be known as the Hawaiian Renaissance. An extraordinary event that attracted worldwide acclaim was the voyage of Hōkūleʻa, which retraced ancient ocean paths from Hawaiʻi to Tahiti, in an open canoe of ancient design and using no modern instruments. This feat came to symbolize one of the greatest achievements of Polynesian civilization. It also produced a search for further cultural identity that created great excitement.

Robert and Wayne as kumu hula in the mid-1970s.

Of this time the scholar Dr. George Kanahele wrote: "What is happening among Hawaiians is also happening in other states, island groups, and countries. Cultural revivals are taking place in the Cajuns

in Louisiana, the Maoris in New Zealand, the Rarotongans in the Cook Islands, the Welsh in Wales, the Bataks in Sumatra, the Filipinos in the Philippines. Wherever there are peoples who feel strongly enough about their identities and legacies, there will usually be strong efforts to preserve and strengthen them. We are not alone in Hawai'i."

However, Kanehele stated, Hawaiian music was in its death throes. There were only a handful of steel guitar players, all of them aging; young people were turned on to rock 'n' roll and could have cared less about Hawaiian music. Outside the islands, the Hawaiian music once so popular throughout the world was also dead. At the same time, Kanahele saw a "revival of neo-traditionalism." This meant incorporating new elements along with traditional values and practices. Because each younger generation brought fresh perspectives, forms, concepts, and words, traditions naturally changed—no matter how imperceptible this appeared to be on the surface. In an uncertain world, change was the only certainty.

At the center of all this change was the young Robert Cazimero, working hard to establish his own *hālau*. In addition, he and his brother Roland and *'ukulele* player Peter Moon formed Sunday Mānoa, a ground-breaking trio that performed in the Hawaiian language. Their songs blended classic and contemporary styles. Robert says that for a long time, Hawaiian musicians were told what was expected of them. It was a double standard. "We knew what we liked, but tourists coming here had their own ideas. The push in the Renaissance, the revival of Hawaiian music, came from being proud of who you were and where you came from." The success of Sunday Mānoa, along with Gabby Pahinui, Olomana, The Sons of Hawai'i, and others, lit a torch that sparked new interest in Hawaiian music. Only years later did Robert find out that their first group was at the forefront of the Hawaiian

Renaissance. "Our music was embraced by the *kūpuna*," he says, "support from different generations, and it helped us to get where we are today."

The Brothers Cazimero

Alongside the realm of *hula*, Robert and his brother Roland formed one of the most successful, beloved, and enduring duos in the history of Hawaiian music. Shortly after graduating from the Kamehameha Schools, their friend Bill Kaiwa asked them to sing background vocals for his Hawaiian album. At the rehearsal, Robert and Roland met guitarist Peter Moon. He had already chosen a bass player for the recording, but when he heard Roland play, Moon quickly made a substitution. Later, Robert and Roland were asked to record instrumental tracks for another album that featured Gabby Pahinui. The "sound" that would eventually become the landmark group Sunday Mānoa was born.

Sunday Mānoa, a groundbreaking trio, performed in Hawaiian language.

Starting Out

The original group included Moon and Cyril Pahinui (one of Gabby's sons) on guitars, Albert "Baby" Kalima, Jr. on bass, and Palani Vaughan on vocals. Soon after, Vaughan left to begin a solo career and Bla Pahinui replaced his brother. After more personnel changes, another trio emerged: Peter, Robert, and Roland. Sunday Mānoa's first album in 1970, "Guava Jam," was the beginning of the Hawaiian Renaissance in contemporary music.

Despite their popularity, Peter Moon decided to break up the group and in 1975, Sunday Mānoa disbanded. Robert and Roland were introduced to Jack de Mello, a Mainland-born composer, arranger, and conductor. He had founded Music of Polynesia, a publishing and recording company that had produced over 200 albums. Jack had heard the Sunday Mānoa albums and wondered how the Cazimeros would sound as a duo.

Almost immediately he put Robert and Roland into a studio to record an album.

The new duo needed a name, so both de Mello and the brothers went home to think about it. The next day everybody returned with the same choice: The Brothers Cazimero.

In 1977, Jack's son, Jon de Mello, began The Mountain Apple Company. Robert and Roland signed on and the Brothers Cazimero had a new manager and a new record label. "It's a great creative and business relationship that has lasted for 35 years, and still going strong," Robert says.

Robert says that without Jon, the Brothers Cazimero would likely not be around today. He has kept the duo working together through the hard times as well as the good and is given the credit for transforming them from backyard *lū'au* performers into the state's leading contemporary Hawaiian group.

Jon De Mello helped transform the Brothers Cazimero into a leading Hawaiian contemporary group.

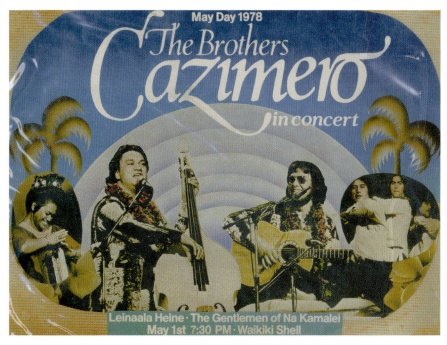

The legendary Brothers Cazimero in concert with Nā Kamalei.

"We work as a team," Jon says, "but Robert and Roland set the course. They have a great sense of where they are and where they want to go. I just keep a close watch on their progress and try to keep the train from falling off the track."

The Brothers Cazimero in a Lei Day concert.

The Sweet Scent of Lei Day

When Jon de Mello went looking for another concert opportunity, he found it with Lei Day. Once again, the Brothers Cazimero inhaled the fragrance of success. "For over half a century," de Mello says, "the celebration of Lei Day had been an important tradition in Honolulu. We decided to add a little spice to it by staging the first Brothers Cazimero Lei Day concert at the Waikīkī Shell in 1978. In the beginning we were only thinking about a single concert, but it was such a success that we've returned to the Shell every Lei Day since."

At the Brothers Cazimero Lei Day Concert in 2003, Robert said, "We're calling this our first year rather than our 26th. We're going back to the beginning." He added that as part of starting all over again, he had sat down and spoken to Roland, and decided that he'd like to go back to the Sunday Mānoa days. "I'd like to be able to talk about it and sing the songs that people keep wishing that Peter, Roland, and I would get together and sing again." By this time there was a parallel with Robert's long career as a *kumu hula*.

The Brothers Cazimero's first Lei Day concert at Waikīkī Shell.

Nā Kamalei and The Brothers Cazimero performing with Honolulu Symphony at Waikīkī Shell.

"When I was taking *hula* from Maiki she said, 'You're going to teach men and that will be it, you will have a school only for men,'" Robert recalls. "I blindly said yes because I loved and trusted her so much. It was kind of the same thing with the Sunday Mānoa. We had no idea what we were doing, we were having good times and in so doing, it formulated what we would eventually become today."

The Gift That Continues Giving

Robert is particularly famed for the beauty of his singing voice, which ranges from a rich baritone to float effortlessly in the fine, high tones of a born tenor. About his older brother and singing partner, Roland has this to say: "His voice is fabulous, I mean he just sings. I am a better singer because I have watched him sing every night. If you're going to back him up, you have to be as good as he is." On the subject of his own gift Robert says, "My voice is a real miracle, and I say that with a lot of *ha'aha'a* (humility), because whenever I've needed it, it's been there." The Hawaiian word, *kahe*, means to flow, like water coming down a waterfall, and that's what Robert and

Roland do when performing together. "We don't have to talk during concerts," Robert says, "we can just feel it."

As masters of their craft, their musical style blends past with the present. The Brothers Cazimero combine chants, dance, and songs of their ancestors to produce a contemporary sound that echoes throughout the Hawaiian Islands and around the world. Longevity is their legacy. Thirty-five years, thirty-six recordings, and one Grammy nomination later, they are still at the forefront of contemporary Hawaiian music. Their journey has included Carnegie Hall in New York City (including a performance with the New York Pops), the Hollywood Bowl, the World Expo in Brisbane, Australia, and concerts in Hong Kong and Tokyo. And the end is nowhere in sight.

The Renaissance of Hawaiian Pride

A story Robert tells about the Kamehameha Schools' Song Contest in the 1970s demonstrates the integration of old and new, and shows *aloha* for the old gods residing in the hearts of Hawai'i's people. "I met a man once who told me that he and I are related through the high priest Hewahewa. He said that Hewahewa dreamed of a man in white, a man from a far country. He saw him bring a man back to life. When he heard of Jesus he thought he might be this man in white, and he thought his power must be good to bring a man back to life. So perhaps he agreed to the overthrow of the *heiau* (place of worship). Hewahewa, they say, wrote the first chant for the new religion.

Top: The popularity of the brothers took them around the world.

Bottom: Paul Luckey on the left, Robert Cazimero, and Frank Kahale in Paris, 1975.

So when we had the song contest, Wayne and I had thirty dancers onstage doing one of the old chants, and a single man dressed in white coming down the aisle through the audience, chanting Hewahewa's *kepakepa* (a rapid style of chant). As he passed, the people of the audience were breaking down in tears. When he reached the stage he walked up to each of the dancers and chanted. Each one kept on dancing, ignoring him, and then left the stage. At the end, he was the only one left."

In 1976, the year Robert's new *hālau* swept the prizes at the Merrie Monarch Festival, a serious challenge to the US Navy occurred. For decades the military had used the sacred island of Kahoʻolawe as a practice site for explosives. Native Hawaiian activists mounted a protest and occupied Kahoʻolawe. One of Robert's hula students missed class to be among those who landed illegally on the off-limits "Target Island."

"I was very uncomfortable with that whole Kahoʻolawe thing," Robert says, "because I didn't know which way I was supposed to feel. We are part of the United States, but we are Hawaiians as well. When I finally decided that I thought that it was better to be Hawaiian than American, then I started to feel guilty because my parents told me that I was wrong, because we have to show loyalty to this country. So then, when it came to sovereignty, I felt uncomfortable again."

Robert is a true Hawaiian at heart.

Roland was a supporter of sovereignty from the beginning. Roland explains, "I used to house the guys that were going to Kahoʻolawe. They would

The Hawaiian Renaissance served as an agent of change.

come up to my house with their Zodiac rafts, make sure they would have gas. Uncle Harry (Mitchell) would come up and we'd talk story. People from Lānaʻi and Maui would stay at my house, thirty people, when I was living up Tantalus. The next day they would hit the water, go Maui and Kahoʻolawe. I would support them by housing them, feeding them; so I knew all about this movement and I'm sort of a soldier." It took almost twenty years for Kahoʻolawe to be returned to the state of Hawaiʻi, ending more than half a century of military control. The Hawaiian Renaissance served as an agent of change. Robert asks, "Why should we have to go to this foreign country who overran our country to ask permission for us to be sovereign, when we already are? We never stopped being sovereign just because they invaded our lands. I guess I've always lived with the understanding that if I just ignore them," he says about legislators, "they will leave us alone. Well, they're not leaving us alone. They are going to squash whatever it is we have that keeps us sane or keeps us Hawaiian. So I support sovereignty now."

Robert's *hālau* is a large part of the "new Hawai'i" contemporary *hula* scene.

During the 1970s, in the local world of *hula* a new, elite class of performers appeared. Old-style dance studios that had taught a limited repertoire of English-language *hula* popular at hotels were a thing of the past. Many teachers had graduated from Maiki Aiu Lake's *hālau* and were part of her "New Hawai'i." The educator Kalena Silva believes that Maiki did the most to change the contemporary *hula* scene. In 1972 she offered a special master class for *kumu hula*, the first time such an opportunity had been available to the public. It attracted a large group of students. Twenty-six eventually graduated as *Papa Lehua*, the first of many groups of *kumu* to emerge from Maiki's "*hula* university." As they established their own *hālau* throughout the islands and elsewhere, Hawai'i was undergoing a rebirth of interest in every aspect of traditional culture. This included Hawaiian language, decorative arts, history and legend, healing arts, food cultivation, martial arts, and more. Although this renewal extended far beyond the scope of dance, it echoed what Maiki often stated as her basic philosophy, "*Hula* is life."

Something else occurred during the Renaissance: the men were dancing again, and the ancient styles of *hula* were being performed again. Although male *hula* was once preeminent, until the 1970s if men danced they were usually considered sissies. This changed dramatically as masculine skill, strength, and beauty came to be sought after. In 1977 George Kanahele wrote: "The most exciting aspect of the *hula* revival is the return of the male dancer to his rightful place. There are far more young male *hula* danc-

The return of the male *hula* dancer was one of the most exciting aspects of the *hula* revival.

ers nowadays than at any other time in recent memory. Male dancers have become a favorite of local audiences."

Yet it wasn't an easy or permanent victory. When the Hawaiian Renaissance of the 1970s ended, certain parts of the revived culture continued, but for whatever reason the tradition of men dancing began to fade away. "It's hard to get men to dance," says Robert. "It's especially hard to find Hawaiian men willing to dance." Although in his *hālau* the emphasis is on being proud of who you are and where you come from, this can be difficult territory.

William "Sonny" Ching of Hālau Na Mamo O Puʻuanahulu says that while the first mention of *hula* in recorded Hawaiian history is of a woman, it was men who performed the ritual temple dances. In addition, regarding the current need to attract and keep male dancers he says, "A lot of them come through the *hālau*, but many don't realize how hard and how disciplined it is. They don't realize that it becomes part of your life. It takes a lot of time and commitment."

According to Mark Keali'i Ho'omalu, who lives and teaches *hula* in the San Francisco Bay area, most men are intimidated by the image of *hula* as being soft and feminine, and the majority of his students are still female. In the opinion of Justin Santos of Fremont, Mark's *hālau* is the first he has seen where men danced really, really strong. Justin says, "I feel my culture is being portrayed in a way that makes me want to be a part of it."

It's words like these that give Robert Cazimero his greatest hope. He has graduated four of his former students and they are now teaching on their own. "Although it's not easy to get men to dance, a new revelation has come along," Robert says, "the sons of my students are dancing for me. But having the kids of my dancers with me makes me want to be a better teacher. That's a legacy."

Just dance, say it, sing it. Be proud of who you are, where you're going, and what you would like to achieve.
—*Robert Cazimero*

Over the next thirty years, Robert mentored hundreds of male students and brought masculinity back to *hula*. Men overcame gender stereotypes to live the proverb: Dare to *hula*, and leave shyness at home. "The whole purpose of the *hālau*," he explains, "was that I wanted to show people

I wrestle with it all the time...There are times when I do not want to get up and dance...to leave that old thought behind and get up there and do it. It speaks well of the phrase that my teacher Maiki Aiu Lake would always say: If the spirit moves you, dance.

—Robert Cazimero

that men could dance *hula* and do so without being thought of as effeminate. Our popularity proves that we've succeeded in doing so."

Another proof of success is that the *hālau* was the subject of a documentary film, *Nā Kamalei: The Men of Hula*, by Lisette Flanary. In her opinion, from tourist kitsch to old Hollywood movies, many people are familiar with romanticized images of women dancing the *hula* in Hawai'i. While few are aware of the sacred traditions of the dance, the role of male *hula* dancers has long been overshadowed by Western concepts of gender and sexuality. The resurgence of male *hula* has changed all that.

Robert says that when the monarchy was overthrown, *hula* went underground and men stopped dancing for decades. Today he states emphatically, "The hiding is over." The future of the dance, he believes, lies in its never-ending past.

CHAPTER 6

KAHIKO: THE OLD SCHOOL

Kūlia i ka nuʻu me ka haʻahaʻa.
Strive for the highest with humility.
—Ancient Hawaiian saying

*K*ahiko (ancient *hula*) is a record and reflection of the times it is created in, and the *kahiko* that we look upon as traditional today was considered contemporary one hundred years ago. Today is a part of life and a part of history and in a hundred years it will be considered traditional *kahiko*. Sometimes everyone forgets what the hula is all about. I've forgotten many times what it really means but as you get older you find that it's real and it's there. The spirit of the *kūpuna* will always be there.

—Auntie Maiki Aiu Lake

How is a dancer trained and why is this important? What are the real differences between teachers? Why are some traditionalists still upset by new trends in *hula*? These often-asked questions are valid. Looking at the background and lives of *hula* masters can offer valuable details on personal standards.

Mary Abigail Kawena Wiggen Pukuʻi

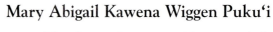

This famous *kupuna* could accurately be called a renaissance woman. She was a scholar and cultural source that has never been equaled. Her many accomplishments included her being an irreplaceable *kumu hula* because of her connections to an ancient past. The following text comes from her daughter, Mrs. Pat Bacon.

Today the young people look upon their Hawaiianess as something that has to be emphasized and accentuated. In my mother's era the Hawaiian identity was something that was understood and even taken for granted. She always knew she was Hawaiian.

Her whole life was centered on the preservation of the traditions of the Hawaiian culture. I think that was her motivation for learning the dance. She was always trying to save this and that by telling the family, "Don't let that get lost." Her mind worked that way. People came up to her frequently because she was fluent in the language and asked her to do a lot of choreography. That's how she began to teach.

She began to teach in the early 1920s. By this time she had moved to Honolulu. My mother had a very inquiring mind and the benefit of that was it pushed her to get to the root of traditions. She graduated traditionally with Keahi Luahine and Joseph ʻIlalaʻole, and their influence on her was that they made her aware of the responsibility of teaching and dancing the hula. If she taught a dance to someone she wanted to see it done properly. She wanted to see the children carry on the culture.

Kawena was a stickler for keeping the hula kahiko the way it was taught to her by her kumu. She was not one to rechoreograph a mele or a dance. If she wanted to create she would compose and choreograph a new mele and dance using the basic motions that had been taught to her by her kumu. She could see that Hawaiʻi was changing quickly and she wanted her grandchildren and the young people of Hawaiʻi to have a record of what once was.

Her advice to me always was to stop, look, and listen. She was always telling me to take my time and not be impatient. Kawena was always writing and scribbling notes wherever she was, whatever she was doing, on whatever she could get her hands on. She used mostly four by six cards but I don't dare throw out anything because I have found notes on things as obscure as the inside flap of an envelope.

My mother felt that the next generation had to have some kind of record of the past so that the Hawai'i that had been wouldn't be entirely lost. She was always saying that she must write this down, there must be a record. She was always encouraging young people like Maiki Aiu Lake and John Topolinski to read and write down everything in regard to Hawaiian culture because if one depends upon their memory, in time it will fade.

Kau'i Zuttermeister

This second notable *kumu hula* taught for over half a century. She is the niece of the late *hula* master Pua Ha'aheo of Kahana, O'ahu. These are her own words and reveal a great deal about her love of *hula* and commitment to it. The traditional style of teaching and learning is worth noting. The strict student-teacher relationship is markedly different from what today's youth is accustomed to.

I began my training in the *hula* at age twenty-seven but I had no real interest in it. My uncle was teaching in Kahana and so my husband Carl drove me to his home one night to watch his classes. For the next six months my husband would drive me down to my uncle's *hālau* each night of the week and I would stand in the back of his *hālau* and watch him teach his *haumana*. Back when I married my husband every wife was taught to listen to her husband, and so it was because of him that I went to my uncle. I was reluctant to learn because parents at that time were always telling their children that the *hula* was bad but as I watched I began to love it. I give all the credit to my uncle and my husband because they saw so much in the Hawaiian culture and the direction that it was going in that I didn't see.

Looking back I think the six months of just watching was the best thing that could have happened to me. When I started to train, the dance came very easily because I already had the background. For three years, class was held every night from six p.m. to nine p.m., and from nine to twelve midnight. Pua's daughter and I would be lectured by my uncle. All my lessons were given verbally and nothing was allowed to be written down. I was not allowed to say anything during my instruction, and I only did what I was told to do. What I enjoyed most about my uncle was his instruction in chanting. He taught us the proper way to breathe and the proper time to breathe. There were many times when the instruction made me feel frustrated and bored. My uncle would put me in front of him and he would say a word from the chant and I would have to repeat it the exact same way he said it over and over again until he was satisfied. One day I asked him why we had to go over one word or one motion sometimes for three hours. He replied that this was how a *kumu* passed on his *manaʻo* (ideas) and power to a *haumana*. When I imitated him I was accepting his *mana*. Moreover, he had taught me my first real lesson in the *hula*–humility. In every art, in every profession, you are taught humility through discipline and the *hula* is no different.

While training with my uncle, I underwent three traditional ceremonies for advancement in the *hula*. The first was an informal ceremony called a *hoʻike* that my friends were allowed to attend. The second graduation exercise was called a *huʻelepo* and this was a more private and serious ceremony than the first. The third graduation was called the *ʻuniki* and this ceremony was complete with all the rituals and traditions of the *hula*. I began to teach in 1929 while I was still training under my uncle. He would take me along with him to Palama Gym where he had at least five hundred students and I would help him teach. I've tried to train my students in ancient *hula* because once you know the language and the basic motions, the *'auana* is easy.

I have never intentionally changed any aspect of the Pua Ha'aheo style. The minute you change or modify what you have been taught then it becomes less pure. That's why I don't change the dances and have kept them intact for fifty years. My uncle told me the only way the culture is going to live is if the dance is kept pure. *Hula kahiko* is all that we have left of our *kūpuna*. It is the only reflection of Hawai'i's past.

Hula is not just dancing and chanting but a deeper spiritual aspect which must be accrued by the student and cannot be picked up in one or two years. In the days of our ancestors, a student would train one five-year period in the *ho'opili* division and one five-year period in the *alaka'i* division. This five-year period was called a *palima* and two *palima* were designated as a *hale 'umi*. The *kumu hula* would *'uniki* each student to the next level and only the best students after completing a *hale 'umi* of training, would be chosen by the *kumu* to be trained as a *kumu hula*.

By custom the *pā hula* would only move up to the level of *kumu hula* after the passing away of their *kumu*. It was an entire social system of selection that hardly exists today. I think what's starting now is that anybody can stand up and say they're a *kumu hula* and if it continues the *hula* will be demeaned and become common. There is a need for the *kumu hula* to come together and set standards and express concerns about what is happening in the *hula* world.

Today it is the dance motions in *kahiko* that command all the attention because the Hawaiians of today do not understand the language. That's why today's motions are so vigorous and exaggerated. The dancers are trying to tell the story totally through the motions of the dance. *Hula kahiko* must be passed down in its entirety from generation to generation because only then does the culture that the *kahiko* is expressing remain intact. *Hula* is a religious ceremony to the Hawaiian gods and goddesses of our ancestors and we can't get away from that. I think creativity can be allowed in the hand movements but the five basic foot movements must be left alone. Each movement symbolizes something important and if they are embellished then we have blurred the lines of our history.

George Lanakilakekiahialiʻi Naʻope

In 1963, George Naʻope co-founded the annual Merrie Monarch Hula Festival held in Hilo. He grew up during the Territorial years before World War II and had to overcome many obstacles in his loyalty to *hula*. By the time he became a teacher, he was somewhat of a rebel who acted as a bridge between the old and new worlds of *hula*. These are his words.

In the old days, everyone was afraid of knowledge being stolen so the old masters would die without sharing it. The different races that live here are part of the future of our culture. I teach Haole, Japanese, Pake, and I used to get scoldings because of it. I want to share because if we don't share these dances they are going to die. My students are all different races but when they dance I know they are Hawaiian.

My first *kumu* was a woman who lived next door to the family in Hilo. She was Edith Kanakaʻole's mother. Her name was Mama Fujii. She was married to a Japanese man. She was a short lady, even shorter than me but she was a master of the *hula*. I studied under Mama Fujii for five years and I will always remember her. I started with Mama Fujii when I was four years old. I'll always consider her my *kumu* because she did the hard work. She was the one that gave me my foundation and basics. The teacher that laid the foundation should be the teacher you give the greatest credit. That's the hardest thing to teach. Mama Fujii, first of all, was very strict. She and my great-grandmother were dear friends and that's the reason I went to *hula*. My great-grandmother told me that our *kūpuna* were *kumu pa'a* so she felt someone else in the family had better learn the *hula*. So it really wasn't a matter of me having a choice about learning or not learning.

I was forced into the *hula* so the more I was taught the more I didn't like it. It wasn't until later that I realized how great a teacher Mama Fujii was. She spoke the language fluently and she had a deep-down rooted feeling for the *hula*. Mama Fujii taught me only *kahiko* but since she was a Christian she only talked about the *kapu* during my training. She would also teach us sitting dances and the *oli* but there would be no *kuahu*. There would only be Christian prayers before and after we danced.

At the age of ten, I went on to Joseph 'Ilala'ole who I stayed with for ten years until he left for Honolulu to become a policeman. He taught me the *kapu* dances and unlike Mama Fujii the training was like the olden days. You had to chant a password to enter the *hālau* and if it was correct, he would answer your chant and let you in.

After graduating from high school, I studied under Aunty Anna Hall who taught me chanting and Aunty Jennie Wilson who taught me *'auana*. Aunty Jennie had a very sedate way of moving her hands. She taught me that the hands tell the story so nothing can be *kuikau*. Every hand movement had to be a definite motion.

My family was poor so I began to teach when I was thirteen years old. This Japanese lady named Mrs. Tsubaki was retiring from the barbershop business in Hilo so she took out all the chairs and let me use her shop to teach. I charged fifty cents a week and with that money I was able to get through school.

I think we need a separate festival of contemporary *kahiko* because I think within its own limits it's great. Then we can have the great young *kumu* of this time create the chants and dances that reflect their era. I've seen tremendous changes in Hawai'i since the 1940s but of my generation there is not one chant that talks about the coming of the airplane, the war, or statehood.

I have tried to teach the *hula* as a classical traditional dance but others are teaching it as a modern, creative dance and are still calling it a traditional dance. Today we are seeing modern day versions of what people think went on in ancient Hawai'i. You have kids coming out who are confused and are calling personally created motions, *kahiko* motions.

(Text for Puku'i, Zuttermeister, and Na'ope is excerpted from interviews in Nānā i Nā Loea Hula: Look to the Hula Resources.*)*

CHAPTER 7

'AUANA, THE NEW SCHOOL

◄◄

Kumu hula of this era often had one foot in the old world and one in the new. They learned, performed, and taught during a time when Hawaiian culture was still devalued, yet they also experienced positive change. From the oldest to the youngest of these masters, all lived to see *hula* reclaim its former position of dignity and inspiration. They also never forgot the sheer fun and enjoyment that can be derived from excellent dancing.

Maiki Aiu Lake

Kumu hula Lake taught for more than forty years. She was beloved and was recognized as a mentor for many of Hawai'i's outstanding young performers and teachers, including Robert Cazimero. In her own words:

As far as my family was concerned the *hula* was a closed book. I came from a straight-laced, Christian family and most anything Hawaiian was not condoned. But in my family was a grandaunt named Helen Correa and to her the *hula* was great people accomplishing heroic deeds in everyday life. In the old days pageants were known as tableaus and she would be called upon by churches to organize Hawaiian tableaus because she knew the protocol. My *tūtū* taught me the mannerisms, the attitude, and the gentleness of the actual dance performances. My first formal teacher was Lokalia Montgomery.

As I studied under her I learned that the *kahiko* could be performed without all the rituals. I didn't have to be afraid and I didn't have to compromise my Christian faith. I went to Aunty Lokalia at fifteen, and by eighteen I was graduated traditionally as a dancer. In those days nobody carried the title of *kumu hula*. They were all musicians or composers or performers and when the elders were no longer around some of the teachers would improvise and put their own feelings into the dance.

After my *'uniki* I was trained by Lokalia to be a teacher and by the time I graduated I had started my family. I would dance in between my family life with Pua Almeida, Lena Guerrero, Andy Cummings, and anybody who needed a dancer when they entertained. In 1946 I was asked by my grandaunt to teach the church members at the Blessed Sacrament Church. I was so grateful for the extra money because now I could buy my children the little things besides only saving money for their education.

I was still a young teacher feeling my way through classes and I would go home and try to remember the things that I was disappointed with in my education. When I studied with Aunty Lokalia there was no paper or pencil so when I'd come home I'd cry at the table trying to retain all that we had been taught. Then my Tūtū Helen would explain the *kaona* to me and she would open up a whole new world. The knowledge of the culture became very real and a part of modern everyday living but how many students had a Tūtū Helen waiting at home for them?

There would be many questions that would be in my mind and my teachers would tell me they would be answered when the time came. Some things were left sitting in the air and my *tūtū* told me if it was meant for me it would be explained. It was a totally different way of learning back then because it was a totally different world and I don't think it would work for the young people of today.

Tūtū Kawena Puku'i told me that we need written instructions these days because we don't speak the language in our homes. So I had a blackboard put in which upset some of my *kumu* but I needed to teach vocabulary in order that my young people could understand what was being taught to them. I started putting everything into book form because I wanted them to be able to take notes home and study. I didn't want them to suffer like I did because if you don't know how to study, learning becomes only stressful. What I've tried to do with my career is standardize the methods of learning the *hula* and give it structure and credibility. The students must do the paper work or they are expelled. I don't consider myself a master but I'd like to believe the *hālau* is carrying on something that my elders have left me.

Nona Beamer has given a title to the *kahiko* the young people of today are composing. She calls it contemporary *kahiko* and I go along with that. *Kahiko* is a record and reflection of the times it is created in and the *kahiko* that we look upon as traditional today was contemporary one hundred years ago. I encourage my young people today to compose their *kahiko* from what they see around them. Today is a part of life and a part of history and in a hundred years it will be considered traditional *kahiko*. Taken to an extreme there are some *kahiko* being danced today that is a combination of styles and innovations. We are seeing *kahiko* today with no history, no tradition, no trace of any original source. It is as if it has arisen from thin air. Sometimes everyone forgets what the *hula* is all about. But you come back and remember. I've forgotten many times what it really means but as you get older you find that it's real and it's there. The spirit of the *kūpuna* will always be there.

Wayne Wai Keahi Chang

Co-founder of Hālau Nā Kamalei, Chang heads one of several men's schools that helped revolutionize the understanding of male *hula* in Hawai'i and abroad. These are his words.

My advice to the young dancers of today is stay with the dance. Don't look for added rewards. Don't look beyond the enjoyment of dance. The dance must be treated as art or else it becomes an endless circle of performances. If you are looking to use the *hula* only as a vehicle for greater reward you are making a mistake. You must be able to dance in a room with no one around and feel the force of *hula*. You shouldn't need anybody to watch you.

My first *kumu* was Aunty Nona Beamer who I first met in 1968 as a senior at Kamehameha Schools. From the start what Nona gave me was a joy for performing and dancing. I was raised on the mainland until I was thirteen so I didn't have a Hawaiian background to fall back on. I did not know the pronunciation and meanings of Hawaiian words so Nona was the perfect teacher for the level that I was at. I think if my introduction to the *hula* had been more accelerated I would have been intimidated by the culture. With Nona if you danced in time to the beat and you enjoyed yourself that was enough. It wasn't important to be perfectly synchronized with the other dancers. If the audience enjoyed the dance and could see you enjoying yourself that's what really mattered.

I studied with Nona for a year and then in 1974 I began my training under Aunty Maiki Aiu Lake. The *hālau* at that time was located on Ke'eaumoku Street and in Maiki's school the *hula* was presented as a form of study and discipline, which was something I had never encountered before. There was a sense of continuity that permeated Maiki's teaching. She stressed that the traditional chants must be protected and perpetuated. She tempered this by encouraging us to create new *mele* and new choreography.

My *'uniki* was held in 1976 and it was a solemn exercise. Many things were not explained but left up to the individual student to interpret as it happened. Frankly the need for definitions and boundaries were unnecessary. The event generated precise feelings without the need for definition.

In 1979 I was led to Kauʻi Zuttermeister who I am still training under today. Aunty Maiki taught me a reverence for *hula* and an awareness that there was a reason for every action in the preparation and performance of the dance but Aunty Kauʻi illuminated the boundaries and protocol with dance and the importance of acting within that framework. I began to teach in 1974 because I wanted to build a "better mousetrap" so to speak. There was a demand for my teaching and I wanted to find out if I could improve upon the teaching styles that were handed down to me.

When I was being trained, the *hula* was my first priority. It came before work, family responsibilities, and personal commitments. This carried over to when I became a teacher and I stopped teaching in 1979 because of this attitude. A true *kumu* is responsible for the actions and behavior of his *haumana*, and after six years I needed to escape the burden of these obligations. I needed to get my world back into a proper perspective.

Leaving Nā Kamalei, which I had co-founded in 1975 with Robert Cazimero, had to be the hardest experience in my career. It meant a total reestablishment and reevaluation of priorities and goals that I had held all my life. Being human I totally enjoyed the pageantry and public response to our work but I began to question the wisdom of using performance as a measure of success and achievement.

The *hula* has become overstated and this has affected the intensity of the interest of the *hula* community that used to exist between 1975 and 1980. The wild crowds aren't there anymore so some *kumu* are choreographing bigger and brasher dances and they are depending on the audience's reaction for their gratification. Most *hālau* have reduced the number of their performances and few of these performances are moneymakers. Ironically, the creative freshness and integrity of the *hula* will be protected and retained because of such economic pressure. *Hālau* will survive and dancers will dance in the future for the pleasure and knowledge of *hula* and not necessarily for public approval or financial gain.

Leinaʻala Kalama Heine

Leinaʻala Kalama Heine, born and raised in Palama, Oʻahu, opened her Hālau Nā Pualei O Likolehua in 1975. She is a featured dancer with the music duo the Brothers Cazimero. These are her words.

Whatever happens from now and hereafter will be looked upon as *kahiko* in the future. There are those that hang on to the past and there are those who only live in the present. In each case there is no movement because the definitions for each side are very narrow. So it's stagnant right now. The present and the past have to coexist with one another if the *hula* is going to move forward.

I don't think a lot of people who knew me before felt I had the ability or the desire to take on the responsibilities that I have now. I do things today that

I never would have done ten years ago. The comic dancer was my role. I was never a straight dancer. I fooled around so much that people wondered about my seriousness. But underneath, the straight dancing was my want. I was a line dancer before I became anything but I could not hold still in a line. I'm one who gets bored fast and I like to make things happen. It was a wonderful feeling to have people laugh with me and at me. It made no difference. Just the fact that people wanted to see more of me was enough. After awhile I started to ask myself where am I going from here, so I started to do some straight numbers and people would laugh thinking I was trying to be comical.

My interest in *hula* started when my mother enrolled me in classes under Ruby Ahakuelo. I was three years old and Ruby would hold class at the YMCA (Young Men's Christian Association) right on Fort Street. Back in the early 1940s, *hula* did not have the interest level that it has today so there was no separation between ʻ*auana* and *kahiko*. Young kids were enrolled at the YMCA or the Department of Parks and Recreation program. I was then taken to my aunt, Rose Maunakea on Kam IV Road and then to the Alma Sisters (Pua and Lei) with whom I stayed on with for quite awhile. At this point I met Joseph Kahaulilio who gave me the incentive for wanting to be something in the *hula*. In the 1940s the *hula* was not the mainstay of being Hawaiian as it is today so it wasn't that important to dance the *hula*. The emphasis at that time was on music and ʻ*auana* and the teachers were not so concerned about the gestures and steps. It was very relaxed, you just came to learn, picked up an implement, and they taught you a *hula*. A student just existed in the *hula* because there was not much knowledge available to students from their *kumu*. Uncle Joe gave me the incentive to make myself more knowledgeable which led me to Aunty Vickie Iʻi Rodrigues. Aunty Maiki Aiu Lake, who is the kumu I studied under, put all of this together and polished away the rough edges.

In 1975 Robert Cazimero asked me to train a few girls for a show, so I began a class made up of fourteen Kamehameha School girls and their friends. Aunty Maiki advised Robert that the boys and girls should be separated and this was how Na Pualei O Likolehua was born. Every day that I go to the *hālau*, I sit down with my ladies and share my past memories and present experiences so that they can have something to draw upon when they dance. Then I have them write up a list of their own experiences because you cannot teach students only on the memories of their *kumu*.

I believe that creativity is important in the traditional *hula* especially if we expect the young people to be attracted to and have a place in the dance. Uncle Joe and Aunty Vickie always told me that repetitious motions become boring and that no two dances or movements should be alike. When you write a new *mele* you are writing from the viewpoint of your lifetime: when you lived, when you trained, when you taught. Your boundary is your death and that life span will record and preserve and express your existence. That is exactly what our master and ancestors did before us and hopefully that's what will happen with the generations after us. The *mele* that we write today are going to be the *kahiko* of the following generations but there has to be limits to creativity as well. Our ancestors have set guidelines for the traditional *hula* but now everyone follows them. So what we have to work towards is a *kahiko* that is traditional but also accessible to people who are new to it.

(*Text for Lake, Chang and Heine is excerpted from interviews in* Nānā i Nā Loea Hula: Look to the Hula Resources.)

CHAPTER 8

ROBERT CAZIMERO THEN

In terms of the *hula* I feel I have shaken this state up. I have opened their eyes, I have kicked them in the pants but you know what? I didn't even know I was doing it.

Nona Beamer was Robert's first *hula* teacher.

I was from a time in the 1960s when being Hawaiian was not important. It was more important to be American. You were trying to get through school so that you could work in Hawai'i or maybe go away to school. The idea of *hula* was foreign. It was an embarrassment to want to do it for all of us. Men's dancing was a novelty and I think to a point it still is today. Men just didn't dance. Kaha'i Topolinski started before me and I remember watching his boys and they were fabulous. Ed Collier was another one who created a male *hālau* years before I even began to train. It took a lot of guts for a guy to get on stage back then. There was an immediate branding of being effeminate and so it was really hard. I'm glad that things have changed a little and I suppose on the surface it looks like it has changed a lot but it really hasn't.

Nona Beamer was my first *kumu* and she was my first contact with the *hula*. I was a sophomore at Kamehameha, guys were just beginning to dance and I was amazed. When Nona was teaching at Kamehameha there was a *kapu* on dancing. No one was allowed to stand up and dance and Nona changed all that. With Nona we began to stand up and actually dance. In my senior year Nona had us choose a song and interview the author. I had chosen Kui Lee and my dear friend Puna Kalama had chosen *Aloha Kauaʻi*, a song written by Maiki Aiu Lake. Puna got her aunt to come to the class and I think I fell in love with her immediately. She sang for us and I accompanied her on the piano and when she left she told me to come to her if I ever wanted to learn *hula*.

Young Robert was one of Maiki's favorite students.

It took me quite awhile to go to her but I started my training in 1968. The class was held one night a week, every Friday, and we would go in and stay for several hours. When I think about it now it was like a dream. I was so taken with her that if she told me to jump off a building with *maile lei* on, I would have gone willingly. Classes were formal in the sense that you gave respect to the teacher and you were there on time. She would start us off with having us sit in a circle and we would talk about what we had learned and what we would be learning. I was with Maiki for seven years with the last five years training as a *kumu hula*. There are things that I did then that I regret now. If you talk to any of my *hula* brothers or sisters they'll tell you that I was a spoiled brat. I was one of the favorites, I knew it, and I played it up. I was real cocky and I suppose I still am.

I graduated traditionally in 1972 and selfishly I felt at the time that I was ready to be a *kumu hula*. But now that I look back I didn't possess the qualities needed. I taught informally in high school with my mother's troupe and with Sunday Mānoa but it wasn't until 1973 that I began to teach seriously. Maiki had graduated me in 1973 as a *hoʻopaʻa* and *ʻolapa*, and in 1974 I was graduated as a *kumu*. There was an opening for a Hawaiian chant and dance instructor at Kamehameha and I applied for it. I taught three classes of girls which my *kumu* called my internship. Next was Nā Kamalei, which was formally founded on Kamehameha Day in 1975.

My definition of *hula kahiko* changes every year. Right now *hula kahiko* is anything that was taught to me before I became a teacher. Now that I am a teacher what I teach is a modern kind of *kahiko*. I consider myself a contemporary *kumu* and I like being a teacher of today. To me *hula* includes the sounds of jackhammers, cranes, buildings going up, traffic. I see *hula* in all of these things. The *kumu* of the past were not any different. They loved what they had but what they had is not what we have today. The question to me is not what is *kahiko* but what is tasteful.

Of the twenty chants I learned from Maiki, the boys have only been taught one. I guess I'm selfish. I won't teach them, it's too precious. It's mine yet and when I'm ready to die or give things up then I'll be ready to share it with them. I think the hardest thing that I had to come to terms with was the gossip and innuendo that was directed at my boys. People mistook my concern and love for my students as something more and I spent a long time trying to please public opinion. When I started in *hula* one thing that I had made up my mind to do was prove that men could dance; that you didn't have to just get up on stage and stomp around with a spear while hitting a paddle against a canoe. There is such a thing as manly grace. But it antago-

From the top, *kumu hula* Moses Crabbe, middle left to right *kumu hula* Karl Baker, Michael Casupang, and Manu Boyd. Robert is bottom center.

nized people and I became such a threat that everybody thought, well, if he thinks he's going to get away with that he's crazy. It's ironic how the young people of today with their own innovations have made my *hula* legitimate. Today they are doing things I would never have thought of or permitted myself to do. Yet I see myself in each of them.

(The above text is excerpted from an interview in Nānā i Nā Loea Hula: Look to the Hula Resources.*)*

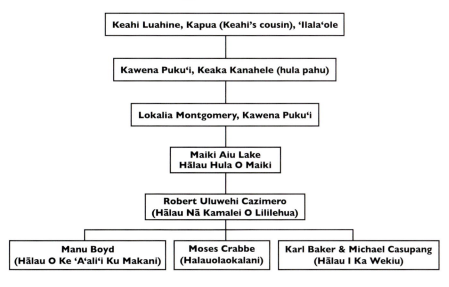

CHAPTER 9

ROBERT CAZIMERO NOW

When you say I am a male *hula* dancer, the majority of people listening to you are automatically concocting their own ideas of what you are supposed to be. I think you have to be very brave to say you dance *hula*. But like everything else in the world, if you can conquer your fear and like what you do, and like yourself, then you truly are the victor.

Lua, or the art of the warrior, is a strong force in male *hula*. If you watch *lua* you will see very similar steps, *hula* steps and also motions that can be used in combat. You know you can pretty much watch any kind of martial arts and to me it looks like dance. The similarity is unquestionable. The end result may be different in its understanding but never in the commitment.

I believe in the gentle warrior. Most people who are students of martial arts know not to start a fight but to prevent it. I like to think that is a part of *hula* too. You know, make love not war. Talk about it, do it, dance about it. But don't be ready for war just yet. The soft *hula* or the slow *hula* is the most difficult to do but is the deadliest. When performing, it is just amazing and beautiful to see what happens.

Once, I saw my *kumu*'s *hula* brother dance and when he danced he moved his hips. Then I saw Mahi Beamer dance and I liked what I saw. To me, this is the difference between dancing and stomping, not that stomping is bad but I wanted my guys to look like they were dancing. There was that movement that took them from point A to point B; you just didn't walk

it, you danced it; you just don't talk about it, you live it. Because of that, the hip movement became singled out and Nā Kamalei was known for that. It took people a while to get over that. Maiki, my *kumu*, would say to me that *hula* should be on the level of ballet. I said, Sure, absolutely I agree, and so I just kept doing what I was doing; until other people started seeing and doing it, this didn't seem too far out there after awhile.

    I would have done anything my *kumu* asked me to do. I was ready to move in with her, my mother was livid. If my *kumu* had said I need you to live with me I would have gone. I thought that is what you were supposed to do. You read those books it says you give up everything and go with your *kumu*. I told my mother I might have to be saying goodbye. She was not happy.

    Everything Maiki said to me became a promise to be a better person, a better teacher for my students. I have been through almost every major crisis any of my dancers have gone through. As *kumu hula*, you are no longer a person. You become an entity. You become all things to all people. We are a family. And because I *hānai*, adopt, them into my family, I make myself available for that. I have had many students knock on my door at 3:30 in the morning, falling to pieces because they are going through a relationship breakup or some parent or grandparent has passed away. I am mother, father, nurse, doctor, counselor, and *kumu*.

A lot of men come through *hālau*, but many don't realize that it becomes part of your life. It takes a lot of time and commitment. If we are going to do something, we all do it together. We all move together. I think I would take it a step further for *hālau* and say that when you become a part of *hālau*, you don't become a part of my *hālau*, you become a part of my family. You are my family.

Once a member of Nā Kamalei, you are part of the family.

CHAPTER 10

THE MERRIE MONARCH FESTIVAL SWAYS THE HEART OF HULA

The internationally famous Merrie Monarch Festival is part of a weeklong celebration named in honor of King David Kalākaua. Traditionally held every April, it is recognized as the world's most prestigious *hula* competition, with people attending from as far away as Japan and Europe. The message sent by the performances of Hālau Nā Kamalei at the 2005 Merrie Monarch Festival was received with unanimous acclaim.

In three decades, the efforts of the *hālau* had come full circle. After their stunning win in 1976 of the *kāne ʻauana* award, just one year after being formed, Hālau Nā Kamalei won top honors for *kāne kahiko* (traditional) chant, *kāne ʻauana* (contemporary) song, and the Festival's overall performance award. Although they had expected to place well, it was unusual for a men's *hālau* to be chosen the best overall.

In the 1976 Merrie Monarch Festival Nā Kamalei won the *kāne ʻauana* award.

When Nā Kamalei members received their trophies, in front of the judges, peers, and a screaming crowd of several thousand, Robert announced, "In a lot of things in life, you work hard and don't get a nod. This is more than a nod. It's humbling, it's outstanding." Then he looked out into the audience and tipped his cap.

About this multiple win Robert says, "I was surprised, I was shocked, I was embarrassed. The *hālau* brothers knew it. I think I am doing it for them, and they are all doing it for me. In the merging of this respect and love for each other, it supersedes the whole idea of competition." In reference to breaking his own rule of entering Merrie Monarch only every 10 years he adds, "I really only came back for them." He wanted to give all his students the chance to celebrate the *hālau*'s 30th anniversary there, especially as there were two men still dancing from the original 1975 group.

In 2005 Robert said that after thirty years in *hula*, "It really didn't matter if we won or not. Even when we lost in the past, I thought we 'won,' because I've learned to lose gracefully, especially in the public eye. But actually winning this year is something so dear—I really don't know how to react. I get embarrassed. It was a wonderful victory because we're not 19-year-old bucks anymore." In a thoughtful mood he continued, "A teacher still learns, day to day. One of the most important things I've learned is that everybody is a teacher. I've learned some of the most important lessons from my students, and some of them don't know this. I've been teaching long enough, gone through generations, and remember things from thirty years ago. Some of the guys in my *hālau* have been with me so

Although winning was not the goal in 2005, Robert and his *hālau* swept the awards in both the *kāne kahiko* and *'auana* divisions as well as the Festival's overall performance award.

long they are grandparents. As a teacher now, I'm experiencing again what these guys, myself included, went through years ago."

Robert also had special words for his *hālau* brothers: "I felt good just coming here, being with my students, especially my students who are teachers now. I am really more happy for them than for myself. I never thought it would come to this." Just before the *kāne kahiko* award was announced Robert was on his feet, pointing a 'you-da-man' gesture at competitors and former students, Karl Veto Baker and Michael Casupang of Hālau I Ka Wekiu, who placed second. Again

Robert rose to his feet when former student Manu Boyd and his Hālau O Ke A'ali'i Ku Makani received an award in the women's division. Then one of Robert's students asked, "Where do we go from here?" He answered, "Pana'ewa (where the *hālau* was staying) to party, and then tomorrow is another day."

Later Robert had more reflective comments. "Mentally," he said, "it was a real chore to prepare for Merrie Monarch. Competition was no longer what it was like a few years before. We had set a standard in the new style of competition. Precision was more important than feeling. I am a strong advocate for how it feels more than how it looks. Making motions and deciding on the songs to do, it is very tricky in any kind of competition. In life, any decision you make is tricky, because it can lead anywhere."

Nā Kamalei performing in the 2005 Merrie Monarch Festival.

On the left, former students, now *kumu hula* Karl Veto Baker and Michael Casupang.

MERRIE MONARCH...

A. Merrie Monarch 1979
Kahiko: Healoha No Nā Pua

B. Merrie Monarch 1988.

C. Alvin Knute Hideki "Gunnie" Hanzawa

D. Merrie Monarch 1999
Kahiko: Manu 'O'o

E. Merrie Monarch 1999
'Auana: Hapa 'Ilikini

F. Brian Keola Kamahele

G. Merrie Monarch 2005
'Auana: Kona Kai 'Opua

H. Merrie Monarch 2005 close up.
Dean Kida, Weylin Hokuton,
Kaulana Vares, Brad Cooper

I. Merrie Monarch 2005

CHAPTER 11

THE GENTLEMEN OF HĀLAU NĀ KAMALEI

'Ohana

The Hawaiian word ʻohana means family, in the sense of an age-old tradition and ancestral way of life. Hawaiians believed that ʻoha, or taro corm, was the root of origin, and that members of the ʻohana, like taro shoots, were born of the same root. In ancient times makaʻāinana (commoners) and aliʻi (chiefs) depended on each other for food and protection. In the words of a traditional proverb: You are a chief because of your people.

One of the Christmas gatherings with Hālau members.

O is the foundation, ʻoha the root, and ha is breath, the essence of life. The concept of ʻohana is about making a physical, spiritual, and intellectual connection to each other. This is done in a way that helps us to carry out our responsibilities as part of a family unit with a sense of lokahi (togetherness). Ancient Hawaiian children grew up in a world where people not related by blood were considered part of the ʻohana as extended family. To Hawaiians, it didn't matter if you weren't a blood relative, only that you were loved. Today it's not unusual for tūtū, grandparents, to live under the same roof as their children and grandchildren. Aunties and uncles—whether close relatives or friends—raise children as well, because *'ohana* extends far and wide. A group of close friends can be members of your *'ohana*. This is the essence of *aloha*, which is extended to all people without restraint or motive. It is our Hawaiian legacy, and is at the center of Hālau Nā Kamalei.

Here, in their own words, are the Gentlemen of Nā Kamalei.

Brad Cooper
Hālau brother since 1975

I made a friendship with Robert through music. When I got to Hawai'i and went to the university, they were having auditions for University Singers and that's when I met him. He was attending the University of Hawai'i at the time and he told me he was starting a *hālau* and they were meeting at Kamehameha Schools. At that time, I was coaching gymnastics and Robert stopped by the gym after school. I used to kid him and I'd say, "Oh! Let's jump on the mat and I'll teach you a back flip." One day he said, "No I have a better idea, let me teach you *hula*." I showed up for practice and one of the guys started to play the *pahu* drums. The men began dancing and I was just watching that strength and the sound of the *pahu*, and I figured it was something I wanted to try. I wanted to be a part of that.

They call Nā Kamalei the mature *hālau*. I've been with them for thirty-one years. More than half of my life has been with the *hālau*, and through the years Robert has been teacher, brother, and now, father, even though we're the same age. I have a connection with Robert. He's been a great *kumu hula*, a source of knowledge for us, but more than that, he's been a good friend. He's watched over us, taken care of us, and has always been there.

Hula has guided my life. Because of my love for these islands, I wanted to learn everything about this place. I studied the culture and now I teach social studies at Kamehameha Schools, a school for Hawaiians. In 1995, I was part of the crew of Hōkūle'a that sailed to Tahiti. What it boils down to is *hula* is life. You wake up in the morning and it's one of the first things that comes to your mind. There's something about *hula*, whether it's just thinking of the others in *hālau* or smelling the flowers when you first get up, hearing the rain. You become much more in tune with your environment, you are more tuned into the beauty of these islands. You become closer to that part of life, it becomes a part of your life. It becomes a part of you.

In *hula* competitions, a lot of times, people look for the glory, the win, the awards, but to me, the journey is what is most important. It's how you've prepared, how you have become closer with your family. Especially for somebody my age, the aches and pains from rehearsing and dancing and sometimes getting out there and knowing that maybe today, I'm not going to be able to perform one-hundred percent. I've been pulled out of competition lines many times. Maybe I wasn't dancing up to expectation. Most people don't know, but Merrie Monarch has an age limit. Once you turn fifty-six, you can no longer dance there. It's in the rules. That's why the year we won, I knew it was going to be my last Merrie Monarch, time to hang up the raffia. I really wanted to be a part of it and make the line. For a while I was taken out, and then I worked my way back in and then I was taken out again, and I worked my way back in again, and was able to be a part of the dance and everything that *hula* means. Like Hōkūle'a, that's the idea of the voyage. Preparation was the important thing. I just wanted to say that I'm fifty-five years old, and I can still dance.

Kaipo Hale
Hālau brother since 1975, Kōkua

In 1975, Robert invited me to dance, when he was co-teaching with Wayne Chang. I danced for five years, then in 1980, I decided to become a *kōkua*, a consultant for the *hālau*, and I've been one ever since.

Hula is a form of expression. In ancient Hawai'i, men were the original dancers and I think the message behind it is saying leave your inhibitions at home, leave all your shame behind. When you come to *hula*, focus on *hula* and focus on the art itself, a dance that is so culturally grounded in ancestral knowledge, history, language, storytelling, motions, all of that. Dare to *hula* means don't be afraid to make mistakes and learn because in the *hālau* you're there to learn and your focus is the *hālau*. Your *kumu* is your *kumu* and he or she directs, develops, and nurtures the *hālau* style so that you perfect that style to the point where she then decides, I think you're ready now to carry on by yourself, to 'ūniki, or graduate, whether it's to the status of a *kumu hula* or an 'olapa, dancer.

The most important thing that I've learned over the past thirty years now is that change is good. The other thing I've learned is that *hula* becomes embedded in every dancer who comes through this *hālau*. Even if you're not dancing anymore, you're still part of that.

Styles change, there are still the basics, but new pieces of work come in and the *kumu* has a decision whether he or she wants to incorporate traditional styles into some new styles. I think Robert has always maintained and always managed a strong level of tradition and traditional style of dancing, but he has an incredible flair of integrating contemporary into that traditional foundation so that kind of change—many people, they kind of look back—and they step back to take a look at it, and say oh, it's different, but still there's the element of tradition in the dancing that has never been lost.

So change is good, you have new members coming into the *hālau*. You have to go through the same rigorous routine in order for them to step up to the *hālau* status where these gentlemen are right now. It's part of their training that comes along and a lot of that change will occur in their lives as they begin those very first steps in entering the *hālau* for the first time. That happened to me when I first entered. I was twenty-four and I saw a lot of changes. One *kumu* leaving and then Robert taking on the sole responsibility of stepping up and taking full reign of this *hālau*...and he's done so brilliantly over the past thirty plus years.

Everyone comes from a different background, but within the *hālau*, the concept of *'ohana* is that every member is a contributing member. The *kumu* is the focus and senior member, historian, trainer, and teacher, so your whole focus is on him. The *'ohana* concept is that everybody takes care of each other. If you have *pilikia*, problems, you take care of the *pilikia*. You have questions, you throw the questions out front and everybody addresses the questions and issues. Like a family, you address the issue openly.

These gentlemen trust each other instinctively, intuitively, honestly, spiritually, mentally and so *'ohana* and trust are integrated almost always, but of course the *kumu* has the last say. But, I've seen these gentlemen mature so much now that Robert can go and leave the *kuleana,* or responsibility, to these gentlemen and they can follow through when he's away. Many *hālau* don't have that. The *kumu* goes away and everything just falls apart and they have to wait till the *kumu* comes home. No, Robert just delegates *kuleana* amongst the members and they carry on.

When you think of the word, the Hawai'i concept of *kōkua* is to help, but it's really helping without being asked to help. My role as a *kōkua* is to provide any form of support that Robert and the boys may need—fundraising, writing music. They perform a lot of the songs I write. If the guys want to talk story about personal issues, it's all part of *'ohana* and trust, and all part of being a *kōkua.* I'm always there for them.

Manu Boyd

Hālau brother since 1978
Kumu hula, Hālau O Ke 'A'ali'i Ku Makani

I joined Nā Kamalei when I was in high school, at the start of my junior year. I was invited to attend because I was taking a *hula* class at Kamehameha. It was called Hawaiian Chant and Dance, taught by Wayne Chang. At that time Robert and Wayne were co-founders of Nā Kamalei but since then Wayne has left to do his own thing and Robert continues on.

I still consider myself a member even though I graduated, and I am still close to the other guys. When you become a member of Nā Kamalei, you are always a member. People very rarely leave his *hālau.* You become a member of his family. His siblings come to know you, his cousins will come to know you, his nieces and nephews and other family come to know you. I consider myself part Cazimero because I grew up with them since I was fifteen years old and it is where I've spent the majority of my life.

In our world, most of the people who are involved in *hula* will not teach. We are not authorized to teach unless given permission by our *kumu*. In my later years in Nā Kamalei, I gained knowledge in Hawaiian history and culture and other areas in language and poetry. In our world and the world of the *hālau*, in order to start your own school, you need to go through training and ceremonies in order for that to happen—to be culturally and spiritually ordained as a source, or *kumu*. In Hawaiian, *kumu* means source.

I did not plan to open my *hālau* at all, even after going through the ceremonial graduation. Actually, other people encouraged me to teach so I talked to Robert, my *kumu*, about it and he determined that it would be a good thing. I had planned to start out teaching just women and I opened my own *hālau*, Hālau O Ke 'A'ali'i Ku Makani, in October 1997. The same month I started at Nā Kamalei in 1978 is when I started my own *hālau* 19 years later. October is a significant month for me.

I thank my lucky stars for my *kumu*. Most of the things that I do today are because of his influence. I think that more and more as a teacher I find that I am increasingly like Robert. He has refined his teaching style. His life philosophies have also refined in that he can make very simple statements that are very strong and impactive. One thing that he taught me that I find myself repeating to my own students today is that both the success and the transgressions within the framework of the *hālau* are a reflection of your *kumu*. In other words, we can't take credit for only the good, we have to take credit if things are not done well. I work very hard to instill in my students a sense of responsibility so that whatever they do is not only a reflection of me but also a reflection of my *kumu*, Robert.

As for the future, I think I want to take a little bit of time and step away from *hula*. I want to go delve a little bit deeper into certain traditions. The *hālau* is ten years old and we are ready to move on to a higher level of *hula*. I am just tired of the rat race. You can spend three months just working on Merrie Monarch. By stepping away for a couple of years I can spend more time on enriching chants. I also hope to produce more music. I have a lot of songs that I have written that I am waiting to teach and share. I want to go a little deeper, to dig down and see what happens.

Kyle Atabay (*Boongie*)
Hālau brother since 1984

In Hawaiian, Nā Kamalei means "*lei* of children." When children are young, they put their arms around you, it's like wearing your child as a *lei*. When you are a teacher, you look at your students as your children, and wearing them as *lei*, meaning, when you wear a *lei*, there's a lot of *kuleana*—responsibility—that comes with it. You don't just put a *lei* on and then toss it to the side afterwards. Once you wear it, it becomes a part of you. And so that idea of "from a *lei*," you take care of that child like it was your own and nurture it to its full development.

I think *hula* is definitely about making a statement. The idea of "daring to *hula*" is really daring to speak, daring to share your story. Daring to *hula* and leaving the shame at home is like anything else. If you're not confi-

dent in what you do, then you may as well stay home because you've got to be confident and strong in whatever statement you're trying to make.

I went to Merrie Monarch in 1989 and 1999 and the preparations for those were nothing compared to 2005. That year, we went with a purpose: to celebrate thirty years of Robert's teaching and also to bring "real *hula*" back to Merrie Monarch. There was a lot more at stake. Knowing that it was our 30th year, we just wanted to go and have a great showing.

The name of the chant we did the night of *kahiko* was called "Kahikilani." It was written by Frank Kahala, one of our *hālau* brothers. He wrote many different chants, but this one in particular we wanted to do. Frank knew the story of Kahikilani and wrote the chant in Hāna. When he left the *hālau* back in 1980 to start his own school, he gave Robert a few chants, and this was one of them.

As the story goes, Kahikilani went out surfing and saw this beautiful woman and he fell in love with her, but she belonged to someone else. When her suitor found out that Kahikilani was looking at her, he was turned into stone as punishment for longing for her. The chant talks about that area where Kahikilani was an *aliʻi*. It is said he was turned into stone. We went down to Bully's house to that area of the North Shore called Paumalū. We found out from Bully's father that the stone is right above their house. From Bully's front yard, if you are looking at the mountain, you can see the stone that is supposedly Kahikilani.

It was very emotional the night we did *kahiko*. After we finished, I went into the back room and broke down and cried. I have never felt that kind of emotion before. It was overwhelming. Before we got to Hilo, we already knew what we were doing was special, and the journey that we had taken to get to that night was incredible. Before we went on, we got together and said what we needed to say. This is why we are here, remember everything that you've done, remember what brought us here. I ended up in the corner sobbing because when *hālau* performed that chant the story of a stone, we were expressing the desire for love, for Hawai'i, and each other, which is what I think "dare to *hula*" is all about.

Stanley Cadinha, Jr. *(Roller Derby)*
Hālau brother since 1987

When Robert first met me, he started calling me "Roller Derby." At that time, the mid-70s, we still had roller derby rinks. We were talking one night and it came up. That's why he started calling me "Roller Derby." It must be an age thing.

Ever since that time, Robert had asked me to come dance. But it wasn't until 1986, when Brad, one of the guys in the *hālau* got married, that I thought about it seriously. I went to his wedding and the boys got up and danced and I got up and danced, too. After I saw the boys dancing at Brad's wedding, I told Robert, "I'm ready, you let me know," so he called me and I came to *hālau*.

There was so much stigma attached to male *hula*, until the Renaissance. Girls thought if you danced, you must be *māhū*. For me, dancing *hula* is not about being gay or not being gay. It's about being proud to be Hawaiian, being proud of yourself, being proud of who you are. There's no shame in dancing. It's something that's going to perpetuate the culture. When *hālau* started, there weren't that many male *hālau* or men dancing. We have come a long way. I think the public watches the men more. It's a kind of a novelty. How often do you see men? You can have fifty women's *hālau* at the Merrie Monarch and you have nine men's *hālau*. I think there is a lot more pressure on men.

One day in *hālau* Reggie said that some think if you dance you're less than a man, and it's something that has to be settled in the parking lot. We used to go to Hank's Place. You'd hear all kinds of comments from different guys in the bar. Finally, it gets to you and you tell the guy, "Eh, step outside," and that's what happens. You had to go and settle it outside because some guys just didn't understand. Funny thing is, Reggie said that when he danced *hula*, he didn't realize that was a great way to get girls.

To me, *hālau* is about *'ohana*, about family. We know each other better than some of our own family members. When there's a break in rehearsal, Robert will ask us, "What's going on?" We sit in a circle and everyone says what's going on in our lives. When someone in the *hālau* is going through a good time or a bad time, everybody knows what is going on. If somebody is going through a tough time at work or maybe a problem in a marriage or with a girlfriend, *hālau* always steps up to help one another. When a boy's mom died, the *hālau* showed up at the service to sing with Robert. I think that's where *'ohana* comes in. Robert is there for us and we're there for him.

Keola Makaiau *(Bully)*

Hālau brother since 1989

I was already dancing with Lahela Kaʻaihue and *hula* was the furthest thing from my mind. I was more of a nightclub kid. I was out almost every night of the week. When I was in my mid-twenties, I was working at a big nightclub known as the Comedy Corner. Lahela Kaʻaihue was the owner's friend and she would use the dance floor for rehearsals. She would tell me, "Come, come dance," and I told her I could never move my hips like that and do that kind of stuff. She convinced me to do it, so I went in. I think I was dancing with her about a year, maybe two years, when she had twins and decided she was going to focus on her children. She wasn't going to teach anymore so I stopped dancing. About the same time, Robert started a new class. He would visit the Halekūlani often. Patrick, who also danced with me through Lahela, worked there. He told Patrick that since we both weren't dancing, would we like to come to the new class?

Patrick called me and I said, Why not? Let's do it! We went to the new class and started dancing again. That was in 1989 right after the *hālau* came back from Carnegie Hall. That's when it started for me and it has never stopped.

Years ago, *hula* was seen as a woman thing—the whole concept of the beautiful *hula* girls, moonlight, all of that. If you were a guy and you were dancing *hula* back then, it was thought of as a feminine thing to do, like how some think of ballet. For Hawaiians growing up in the country, *hula* was not thought of as something guys did. Everybody in the past who dared to *hula*—all the men—would have just left their shame at home. It's like saying, this is what my culture is all about, this is what I'm going to do, I'm going to dance. These are the guys, hundreds of *hula* dancers, who we owe our thanks to. Back then there were very few male *hula* dancers. There were no other male schools. We owe a lot of credit to those guys for not being ashamed, for just going out and doing what has been part of their culture for thousands of years.

My mother loved watching me dance the *hula*. My father, though, never said anything about it. I don't know if he was ashamed. He was from the old country, from Lāiʻe, a big football star—Kahuku All-Stars. When I was growing up, he wanted me to go to Kamehameha High School. I was the first in the family who had an opportunity to attend Kamehameha, but I wanted to stay at Kahuku—country, through and through. I don't think he expected his son to be a *hula* dancer. But now my father accepts it. He understands the cultural value. Before, he took it strictly for the stigma. Dance as opposed to more manly stuff. When *Men of Hula*, the film documentary of the *hālau* came out, and there was a scene of me dancing, my father turned around and whacked me in the chest and smiled. He has definitely grown to accept it.

The most memorable thing for me at Merrie Monarch was the *oli*, or chant, after we won the *kahiko* award. When a group wins an award, they stand there and chant. Boongie turned around and looked at me to start it, so I began at a very high pitch. When you start high, there are parts where you have to go higher. They said, "We asked you to start it because you are a bass and you start on a way high tenor note." Even Robert noticed it. Everybody laughed, and they never let me forget it. The whole Merrie Monarch trip—the practice, the sweat, the rewards —was all worth it. We had a mission to go out there and work, whether we won or lost. Our mission was about going out there and showing that we can still do it. And we did.

Frank Among

Hālau brother since 1990, Kōkua

Robert asked me in the early 1980s if I wanted to dance. I've always been a big fan of the Brothers Cazimero and the *hālau* from the start, even during their Sunday Mānoa days, but I don't see myself being in front of people. I'm comfortable in the back helping and assisting. In 1990, I moved back to Hawai'i from the mainland and got reconnected with the *hālau*. He asked me to be a *kōkua* and, of course, I said yes. *Kōkua* means help or support, and that's exactly what I do. I worked in the travel industry and because everyone in Nā Kamalei travels so much, I make all the arrangements. I also do a lot of the photography. In fact, one of my pictures was chosen to be on the cover of the *hālau* CD, of Keala, on the RCHNK CD.

In 1993, the entire *hālau* went up to San Francisco to visit Scott, one of our *hālau* brothers, because he had AIDS. That was right before he passed away. We ended up surprising him. It was supposed to be just for a weekend but we ended up staying for two weeks. We decorated his apartment, we put a Christmas tree in every room. Gifts everywhere. It was one big party for two solid weeks and Robert wrote a beautiful song there for Scott, which is on one of the Cazimero CDs. That definitely was the best Christmas ever and one I'll never forget. A few months after that, Scott died.

I like to think of the *hālau* as a family. Of course, Robert is there as the foundation. On one trip to Kohala, Robert wrote another beautiful song while we were there. When I thought about what they were singing, it inspired me to learn the Hawaiian language, finish my degree, and find out more about different cultures, including my own.

I have to say my best memory is from Merrie Monarch in 2005, the year we won. Before we performed, the *hālau* went to the crater for blessings—Halemaʻumaʻu on the Big Island. As we got there and began walking in it started raining really hard. Naturally, I was taking pictures. We usually go there to give back and make an offering, to ask for permission and protection. When we got there and got out of the vans, it was pouring rain—driving, freezing rain—so we took a five minute walk up to the rim, to the edge of the crater and Robert said a chant and offered a *lei*. Right after the chant ended the sun came out really strong and there was a rainbow. It was this strange rainbow, Robert called it *uakoko*, earth-clinging rainbow. It was a rainbow sitting on the earth, just above the ground and it's very rare, so I took it as a sign: the rainbow, visiting Scott in San Francisco. It always feels like that with the *hālau*, rare magical moments.

Alexander Parker *(Alika)*

Hālau brother since 1994

Robert has known my family since I was a kid. My *hānai* mom, my adopted mother, would say to me, one day you're going be a dancer for Nā Kamalei. Then she passed away, well, you know what it is like to lose your mom. Robert remembers this. He came up to me at the funeral and said it's time for me to give him a call. A few weeks later, a friend said to me, Braddah, *hālau* is starting up again and you need to go. She didn't know that Robert knew me. I went to the new members class and Robert smiled and said, you're here. I came to *hālau* because it was my time. I don't know if I was in mourning and needed to find something, or if I was just ready, but I've been in *hālau* ever since.

You know that saying, in your lifetime you can count your friends on one hand? Not true. I can depend on every one of my *hula* brothers. When I came to *hālau* and started to learn who my *hula* brothers were, my love for them grew deep. I can count on anyone for anything at all.

Some people think *hālau* comes first before your family. Some believe that your family comes first before *hālau*. To me there's no separation because my *hula* brothers are my family and I know that if something happened to me, I can depend on any one of them to take care of my wife and my children. They would come to my rescue. It's something that you have to experience. It kind of frustrates us because we cannot explain it but it's something special—out-of-this-world kind of special.

The most important things I've learned in *hālau* are balance of life and recycling. Balance of life means my work and my culture, which is, of course, *hula*. My family supports my career choices and my *hula*. My *hula* supports my family and my career. Balance of life has made me who I am today.

Recycling comes from the Western way of thinking that people feel you need to work to own, to get more and more, but it's the opposite. This whole recycling idea is that you're not carrying the burden of the world. If I carried your burden, his burden, their burden, then it would become so overwhelming. Recycling is about being there to help, to love, to give back, and put back.

For example, when new guys come into *hālau*, we teach them the basics, to do our style of *hula*. Once you take Nā Kamalei into your life, a door opens, and there are so many opportunities that come up that only now makes sense for me. It's like having a child. You don't know what life is like until you hold your first born. I have four kids now and I always tell people that when I first became a father, I asked myself, what did I do before this? What was my life like before my first child? It's the same thing with *hula*—only different.

I don't understand the Western world. Their vision of a *hula* dancer is female, they don't understand why a man calls himself a *hula* dancer and is up there dancing because they only know *hula* to be a female talent. I don't shun away from it because I'm worried about what others think, and I don't want to say, I don't care what they think, because I do care. I want everyone to know that this is who we are. We're not just male *hula* dancers, we are all Hawaiians in spirit. We are Nā Kamalei.

Keala Chock

Hālau brother since 1997

I was fortunate that Robert asked me to dance when I was a junior in high school. I am Hawaiian and I am perpetuating and preserving my culture and learning more about it. I'm the second youngest member and have been dancing in *hālau* for ten years, since I was sixteen. I'm just honored that I can carry on something that my mom did, and my grandparents, too. It's my life.

In *hula*, you have to come with an open mind when you come to practice and when you perform. If you have shame, if you're holding onto things, you're not going to perform well. Your dance is going to be a little rough, a little rigid and it's just basically letting all the inhibitions go and coming forward with a clean, positive mind which you want to put out to people. When you're learning new things, you're a little embarrassed to try it out. Especially for men dancing, it's more so, it's a little more difficult because there's a stereotype that if you're a guy and you dance *hula*, you're possibly gay and so for the guys it's even tougher to do that for *hula*. You just have to leave it all behind and not worry about dancing.

'*Ohana* and trust are two huge words and I think that they are pretty high on the value list in terms of what Robert tries to do with the *hālau*. We are a family. This is not just a *hula hālau*. It is far beyond that. It's building that bond, that family, and part of that is having trust in each other and having trust in Robert and in what he's doing. For me, I mean, I consider these guys my family, all of them.

For me, *hula* has never been about competition and about receiving accolades, it's about a lineage that we represent and a tradition that we carry on. I could care less about what other people think, to tell you the truth, as long as everybody's having a good time in *hālau*, and we always have a good time. We work hard when we work, but we have fun when we need to have fun. I mean it goes beyond just *hula*. We're all good friends. They're a part of my family.

When I first came to *hālau*, I think everybody was sort of testing me to see what I was going to do. I didn't know how to make any kind of *lei* or anything and that was really important you know because here I am, getting into *hālau*, and I had no idea how to make my own *lei*. May Day is our first performance and I'm just freaking out. I called up Bully and said, Hey man, I'm shy about making my *lei* in front of everybody because I no like make 'em all buss up. He didn't know me that well but he came over to my house and just sat in my yard and he showed me how, from cleaning the flowers, showing me how big the flower should be, how tight the braids have to be. Some may think it's just a *lei*, but Bully was willing to drop everything and come and help me. That's *hālau*. I'll never forget that, and I made my *lei*.

Keo Woolford

Hālau brother since 1999

My vision of the dance comes from a proud Hawaiian tradition. There's such a stigma about men dancing because traditionally, in almost every aspect of the dance world, the majority of dancers are women, except in hip-hop. If it moves you, you should do it, because as long as you are not hurting anybody, there's nothing wrong with it.

I took my *hula* roots and transplanted them onto New York soil. I Land is a one-man show that ran off-Broadway. It's a semi-autobiographical story that weaves traditional *hula*, hip-hop, and talk story (an informal and casual Hawaiian voice) into a Hawaiian tapestry that explores the many worlds of the dance. In the show I talk about my first exposure to the *hula* and how I came under the instruction of my idol, who I call the "Hula god." I also describe my fleeting brush with fame as a member of a boy band that almost hit the big time, my descent into drugs and partying, and my rediscovery of the sacred dance that inevitably reconnects me to Hawai'i, my culture, and myself.

The whole concept of what it meant to dance *hula*, because of the stereotypes, took courage to be strong in oneself to not care what anybody

else thought and to just dance. The style that we have is really difficult and it's also very different from any other male style—where the hips are such a huge part of the movement. And to see men dancing with their hips a lot of times brings a connotation of being effeminate. This is the idea that Western ideals have placed on our culture, where in old Hawai'i, no one cared, because it was just something we did. Bravery and self-belief to dance, in this style, with these teachers, took a lot of courage.

I Land is political on many levels: first, in terms of the images of Asian-American and Asian-Pacific males. They are usually invisible, emasculated, or foreign. One of the things that I am so proud of in the show is the explosion of stereotypes about Asian men. In the media we are constantly bombarded with images that portray Asian-American men as asexual, geeks, dorks, subservient to the black or the white man, or that we're kung-fu masters or bad guys. This show does not fit into any of those things.

What I really wanted to do is expose people to my *kumu*. Like many, I consider Robert a significant part of the contemporary Hawaiian Renaissance. I have to pay homage to the *hula* brothers who came before me and I give thanks to the people who kept the dance from going underground.

Every night before I went on stage, I would chant and a couple of friends I made in the cast would come and join in. There was a preparation, a ritual, a grounding that I did before the show. Robert Cazimero choreographed the show, and when he came to see it, he taught us a little answer to the chant, so we would do that before the show. Before each show, I would think back to the chants and I felt an immediate connection, I felt everything was okay. A big part of that had to do with being part of a group, and having a sense of belonging with the *hula*. There was that support, and I knew that I was safe.

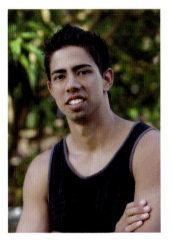

Kaulana Vares *(Kauboy)*
Hālau brother since 2003

They call me Kauboy. Back in 2003, we went to Kohala for Robert's family reunion on the Big Island. Kaipo, one of my Nā Kamalei brothers, started calling me that, Kauboy, and it just kind of stuck.

I don't think that I chose this *hālau*, I think this *hālau* chose me. I'm the youngest, I'm twenty-four now, and I've been here since I was seventeen. I used to dance *hula* when I was younger with Sonny Ching's *hālau* for four years. You know, *keiki* time. When I got older, Robert had a new class and I came out for it. Robert has helped guide us to find out what we want in life. For me, it's being Hawaiian.

My mother has been a *hula* dancer from the time she was a teenager and she became friends with our *hula* brother, Manu. She's been dancing with his *hālau* O Ke ʻAʻaliʻi Ku Makani, from the very beginning. When he started his *hālau* ten years ago, my mom was one of the first members. It seems only natural that we stay within the same *hula* line and learn from the same teachings. My mother and me, our *hula* is synonymous with each other. It's all part of being Hawaiian, and the way our family is. My brother sings with the Hawaiʻi Opera Chorus and that kind of defines him, being involved with his culture. I have another brother, the second oldest. He's always reading, looking into the political side of Hawaiian history. That's the way he connects himself to his culture. My third brother, he's still finding his way. One day he'll connect to his "Hawaiianness."

As for me, I just connected to the 'āina, the land, and the stories that have taken place over history. We have to tell our own stories, people can't be telling them for us. You could say the blood that runs through my veins is pretty much the same blood that's been shed on this land. It all connects.

I think it's definitely a lot easier than it was twenty or thirty years ago to be a male *hula* dancer. It's probably not as hard. In Western culture, it's not really a place for men to dance *hula*, but there's no shame. I do what my *kūpuna* tells me. Robert says it's about being proud of who you are and where you come from. I believe that because even though we live in Honolulu one of the most populated cities in the United States, I still feel it's a Hawaiian place. *Hula*, Nā Kamalei, living in Hawai'i—it makes me proud to say that I'm Hawaiian.

CHAPTER 12

THE WORLD COMES TO HULA

*I*n *hula*, a universal embrace comes as part the territory because the art of the Hawaiian dance knows no boundaries. *Hula* spans continents, its reach spreading to all corners of the globe, its appeal ultimately leading the world to one revered locale—its place in the past. Some believe *hula* is about being Hawaiian, others believe it is about feeling the spirit of Hawai'i, the culture and traditions. This is certain: *hula* is about respect and love for our heritage, our *kūpuna*, the *'āina*, and one another. It is about feeling the heartbeat of the Hawaiian people. As a result, the ripple effect that *hula* has created is, indeed, far-reaching.

Although Patrick Makuakane lives in San Francisco, his heart can be found very close to his passion: *hula*. A Nā Kamalei brother since 1975, and *kumu hula* of Nā Lei Hulu I Ka Wekiu, he says that Northern California has the second-highest concentration of Hawaiians outside of Hawai'i. "When I first started *hula* in San Francisco, people in Hawai'i looked at us like, 'Oh, how cute—those people on the mainland are trying the *hula*.' But over time we've really made a name for ourselves, and now it's like we are part of them. We, too, are perpetuating the process, and I think that we are doing things that are as valid as they are." Part of his process involves taking modern music and adding traditional moves. "I

On the right, *Kumu hula* Patrick Makuakane

take artistic license," he says. "I don't take old chants and old dances and modernize them. I leave them alone." He incorporates *hula* movements to form a new vocabulary that, for him, is very expressive.

"We're seeing a phenomenal growth in the *hālau*, not just in California but farther east—in Las Vegas, Salt Lake City, Colorado, Arizona," says Amy Kuʻuleialoha Stillman, an associate professor of music and culture at the University of Michigan at Ann Arbor, and the director of its Asian/Pacific American Studies Program.

In 2001, at the World Conference on Hula, more than 1,500 *hula* enthusiasts joined forces on the Big Island of Hawaiʻi to celebrate the history, genealogy, and ancient chants of *hula*. Kekuhi Kanahele, executive director of the Edith Kanakaʻole Foundation, said: "We began to realize the worldwide extent of *hula* when we received a registration from Egypt. Then the registrations kept coming—from Iran, Japan, Mexico, and all over the United States."

In France, nothing communicates love quite like the language of *hula*. "Our *hālau* functions like a large extended family," says Sandra Kilohana Silve, *kumu hula* of Hālau Hula O Mānoa in Paris. One of her artistic ambitions is to educate a European audience about Hawaiʻi's history and rich heritage. She shares diverse *hula* styles with her *haumana*, emphasizing an understanding of the islands' history. "I often return from Honolulu with boxes of *ti* leaves, rare in Paris, to teach my *haumana* to make *ti*-leaf skirts. We treasure and *malama* the leaves for weeks in the refrigerator." She believes in blurring the lines of continental boundaries. Silve says: "We now grow *ti* plants between the radiator and the French antiques."

The Dutch-Indonesian *hula* dancers of Hālau Hula ʻO Maiʻana were born in the Netherlands and raised with a mixture of Indonesian and Eu-

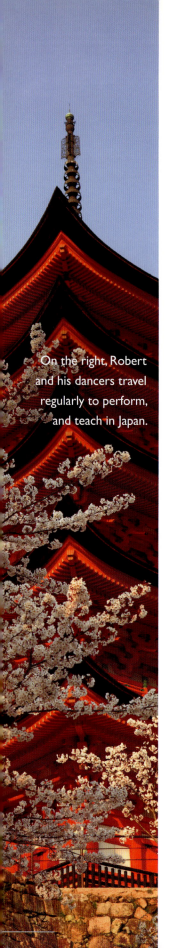

On the right, Robert and his dancers travel regularly to perform, and teach in Japan.

ropean influences. They often feel lost without a culture they can call their own. But when they dance the *hula*, they are exactly where they belong. "We are one with the people, the land, and the culture. We connect with the emotions of the land we call home—Hawai'i."

The members of Hālau Hula Fa'arere 'Ike in Mexico believe the international wisdom of *hula*. By preserving Hawaiian culture and studying the philosophy of *aloha*, they are able to pass on the knowledge as it was taught.

"Our *hālau* believes that if we work together, united toward a common goal, we can change the world."

In Japan in the 1980s, *hula* courses were aimed at housewives, offered through community cultural centers as a form of aerobic exercise. Today there is a much more sophisticated approach. Approximately 250,000 Japanese *hula* students learn the dances of Hawai'i in 220 *hālau hula*. Teaching is done through the hierarchical guild system known as *iemoto*. According to Amy Ku'uleialoha Stillman, "Many *hula* troupes in Japan are now viewed as branches of the Hawaiian master instructor's *hālau* in Hawai'i, and lower levels of students are taught by assistant instructors. One teacher had twenty-five assistant instructors throughout Japan, and another teacher had thirty assistants teaching at cultural centers, while she herself only taught instructors. *The Honolulu Star-Bulletin* reported in 1998 on former Honolulu resident Anthony Kahoku Tauvela who directs a *hālau* in Tokyo with

139 students; his nine assistants instruct 780 additional students in Tokyo, Kyoto, Osaka, Kobe, and Okinawa. In the 1998 World Invitational Hula Festival, all three instructors of the troupes competing from Japan listed a Hawai'i-based co-instructor."

Hide Kalanimoku of Aoyama, Japan, feels what is most important about the *hula* is the fragrance of *aloha*. "The first time I put on a *lei* I was on the island of Hawai'i, where my teacher, Robert Cazimero, made one of *palapalai*, ginger, and *'a'ali'i*. What was astonishing was that we picked the materials as we walked along the path, and as we sat on a bench, with the sound of 'Akaka Falls in the background, Robert made the *lei* in an instant. I have a special attachment to the Hawaiian *lei*, and it has been the foundation on which I have based my life. It is a necessary part of *hula*. These days, many dancers use imitation *lei*. I believe fresh flowers and greens should be used. This is especially important for the Japanese. Since we are from a different culture, we should take care to honor and respect the sacredness of the *hula*."

The fragrance of *aloha* is spread through the love of the dance—*hula*.

CHAPTER 13

HULA IS LIFE

When asked about the future, Robert Cazimero offers a look of childlike wonder. After winning everything at Merrie Monarch in 2005, more than thirty years as *kumu hula*, and a lifetime of *hula*, people ask if he is going to retire. "I wonder if that's what I'm supposed to do, but that's not what I want to do. I have years to teach, many more concerts to give."

Back in 1982, a few days before opening night in the Monarch Room at the Royal Hawaiian Hotel, a designer said that since the Brothers Cazimero had made it to the top by performing at the legendary hotel, where would they go from there? Robert told him that later he was going home to Kalihi, because that was just as good.

"After the *hālau* won," he says, "I went to Brazil for a vacation, then we held a garage sale in Kaimuki to raise money, and now we're going up to the Pali to pull weeds. The weeds are growing, we have to pull weeds."

In 2010 the Brothers Cazimero performed with a group of dancers at the Hawai'i Theatre.

Leinaʻala Kalama Heine has been performing with the Brothers Cazimero since the very beginning.

Photo by Wayne Iha

His journey continues. Robert says that whether they're headed to Japan or holding a *hula* workshop in Portland, the greatest lesson he's learned about traveling is that it makes you appreciate home. "People in Tokyo, Umbria, Seoul—they expect certain things of you if you are Hawaiian. Tell me who you are, because they know who they are. When I see other cultures, I want to come home and learn more about my own."

Ramsey Taum, a University of Hawaiʻi instructor of Native Hawaiian practices and one of the first *hālau* brothers of Nā Kamalei, says this about its special place in the world: "Every place or travel destination has a story, a persona, customs, and traditions. The spirit of *aloha* is one of those characteristics that can't be bought or sold. Sense of place helps to define the relationships we have, as well as how we treat one another."

It's a spirit that isn't only measured in words, but by actions, and for Robert Cazimero, his spirit encompasses both. Whether choreographing the rhythms of male *hula*, performing as one half of the Brothers Cazimero, or giving voice to Hawaiian culture, he is most at home when blending lasting gestures into a oneness that celebrates life's dance.

The *hālau* is one with Robert. The brotherhood extends beyond the bloodline.

As a musician and *kumu hula*, he sums up everything in a simple, powerful statement: *Hula* is life. "It expresses everything we see, feel, hear, smell, taste, and touch." He believes that the best thing Hawai'i can do is to let the world know that we have a dance form. What the world can do is let Hawai'i know that dance is universal. People are drawn to *hula*, not just the *hālau*. That's the way art is, he says, it's inviting; it's enticing.

"It brings tears to my eyes."

HULA IS LIFE...

A. An HNKOL fundraiser at the Hilton Hawaiian Hotel.
Scott Galuteria, Brad Cooper, Robert Cazimero, Keala Kamahele, Doug Hoku Wong.

B. 1999 Merrie Monarch after-party at Moses Crabbes' Hālau in Hilo.
Charles Manu Boyd and Michael Lanakila Casupang dancing.

C. HNKOL 34th breakfast birthday party in Kailua, Oʻahu.
Hauʻoli Medina, Barry Ki Quilloy, Robert Cazimero, Kyle "Boongie" Atabay.

D. HNKOL 34th breakfast. Alvin "Gunnie" Hanzawa, Stan "Spike" Cadinha, Daniel Nahoʻopiʻi.

E. Pulling *kalo* at the Makaiau family *kalo* day in Paumalū. Dean "Nahoa" Kida, Robert Cazimero.

F. A concert at Kahilu Theater, Waimea, Hawaiʻi Island.
Charles Manu Boyd, Keola "Bully" Makaiau, Robert Cazimero.

G. 2009 HNKOL Fundraiser at Chai's Island Bistro, Honolulu, Oʻahu. Robert Cazimero.

H. Pan Pacific Hula Exhibition, 2009. Tokyo, Japan, with good friends.

CARRYING ON THE LEGACY...

A. The Papa Maile walks into the ocean for a ceremonial *'au'aukai*. Lead by Kahu Charles Ka'imiokahelelani Padua.

B. HNKOL after the *puka* ceremony for Brad Cooper and Kyle Atabay.

C. Brad Cooper gets his *lei hulu*.

D. *Honi* from *kumu hula* to new *kumu hula* Kyle Atabay.

E. Kyle Atabay gets his *kihei*.

F. Kyle Atabay and Brad Cooper do the "Trilogy" as Po'o Pua'a Edward Bruce Hanohano and *kumu* watched.

G. Robert Cazimero does an *'oli* as three *kumu hula* of the Papa 'A 'Ali'i, Karl Veto Baker, Charles Manu Boyd and Michael Lanakila Casupang, watch.

BIBLIOGRAPHY

Adams, Wanda. "Cazimero Celebrates Return to Merrie Monarch with Overall Title." *Honolulu Advertiser*, April 3, 2005.

———. "Gallant Effort Lifts Merrie Monarch." *Honolulu Advertiser*, April 4, 2005.

———. "Hālau I Ka Wekiu wins overall Merrie Monarch prize." *Honolulu Advertiser*, April 15, 2007.

Ariyoshi, Rita. Ed. Lee Puakeala Mann. *Hula is Life: The Story of Hālau Hula O Maiki*. Honolulu, HI: Maiki Aiu Building Corp., 1998.

Berinobis, Shari. *The Spirit of the Hula*. Honolulu, HI: Bess Press, 2004.

Blumberg, Jess. "A Hip Tradition." *Smithsonian* August 1, 2007.

Enomoto, Catherine. "Cazimero Brothers Mark 20 years of Song and Celebration." *Honolulu Advertiser*, April 28, 1997.

Flanary, Lisette Marie. "Patrick Makuakane," *American Aloha*. <http://www.pbs.org/pov/pov2003/americanaloha>.

Hale, Constance. "The *Hula* Movement." *The Atlantic*, July 2002.

Harada, Wayne. "If It's May Day It Must Be the Caz." *Honolulu Advertiser*, April 29, 2005.

Hopkins, Jerry. *The Hula.* Hong Kong: Apa Productions (HK) Ltd., 1982.

Hula Men: *Endangered Species.* CBS News, April 24, 2003.

Kanahele, George. *The Hawaiian Renaissance.* Honolulu, HI: Project Waiaha, (1982), 39.

Klarr, Caroline. *Hula, Hawai'i's Own Dance.* Honolulu, HI: Cultural Resource Management (1988), vol. 21, no. 8, 26-27.

Nānā I Nā Loea Hula: Look to the Hula Resources. Vol. 1. Photographs by Shuzo Uemoto. Ed. Wendell Silva and Alan Suemori. Honolulu: Kalihi-Palama Culture and Arts Society, 1984.

Reynolds, 'Aukai. "What Is the History of Hālau Ika Ka Wekiu?" <http://www.halauikawekiu.com>.

Ronck, Ronn. Celebration: *A Portrait of Hawai'i Through the Songs of The Brothers Cazimero.* Honolulu, HI: Mutual Publishing, 1984.

Sen, Benton. "The Inviting, Enticing Art of *Hula.*" *Spirit of Aloha*, January 2007.

Silva, Kalena. "The 'Ūniki of Maiki Aiu Lake's Papa Lehua." *Biography Hawai'i: Five Lives—Maiki Aiu Lake.* University of Hawai'i: Center for Biographical Research. <http://www.hawaii.edu/biograph/>.

Stillman, Amy Ku'uleialoha. "Globalizing *Hula.*" *1999 Yearbook for Traditional Music*, Vol. 31 (1999) 57-66. <http://www.jstor.org/stable/767973>.

Woodhouse, Jon. "Back to the Beginning with The Brothers Cazimero," *The Maui News*, May 1, 2003.

Woolford, Keo. "Interview with Keo Woolford." *Asia Society*, August 13 2008 <http://www.asiasource.org/news/special_reports/iland.cfm>.

ABOUT THE AUTHOR

Benton Sen was born and raised in Hawai'i. His essays have appeared in *Spirit of Aloha* magazine, among other publications. In 2007, he received a writing award from the Society of Professional Journalists and another in 2008 for an article on Robert Cazimero and Hālau Nā Kamalei, on which this book is based.

Benton has received the James Houston Fellowship from the Squaw Valley Writers Conference, the Walker Foundation scholarship from the Fine Arts Work Center in Provincetown, and a writing fellowship from the Vermont Studio Center. He attended the Nonfiction Writing Program at the University of Iowa and now lives in Honolulu. *Men of Hula* is his first book.